REFLECTIONS OF A MUDMAN

BRIAN MOONEY

WRITING ON THE WALL

Writing on the Wall
Toxteth Library
Windsor Street, Liverpool
L8 1XF

Published by Writing on the Wall, 2025

© Brian Mooney 2025

The right of Brian Mooney to be identified as the Author of the Work has been asserted by him in accordance with the Copyright, Designs and Patents Act 1988.

Design and Layout by Jenny Dalton
Cover Design by Ged Doyle Plastic Design

978-1-916571-24-2

0151 703 0020
info@writingonthewall.org.uk
www.writingonthewall.org.uk

For Girlie

Foreword

If you, your family, or your ancestors were from 'under the bridge' in Garston, or you want to know what life was really like in Liverpool of old, then this book is for you.

Under The Bridge will be one of those places whose name remains synonymous with the image of Liverpool: long, narrow streets, terraced houses, pubs, and pawnbrokers; an area enclosed by the river and the railway lines. At one end, Church and King Street form the village; at the other, the dock gates open to the Mersey and the world beyond.

This is the birthplace and spiritual home of Brian Mooney and his brothers. In this memoir, he reflects on his childhood on the muddy shore, and on a family history in which the tides of global events are distilled into the lives of a working family.

My mother was raised on King Street, in a 'two up two down' with an outside toilet, but the wonders of the seaport which formed Brian's experience meant my mum's house also contained not only a shed full of siblings but a parrot and a monkey brought back by sea-faring brothers.

Brian traces his family history like many others to Ireland. *Under The Bridge* was known to many as little

Wicklow. The Mooney's came from Dalkey, just up the coast. Protestant, and Catholics have coexisted in this city for hundreds of years, along with Welsh Methodists influence. For most of the time, most of the people found more in common than reasons to divide. Although divisions were also present, within families and communities, and Brian does not shy away from some of the family consequences of this.

From experiences in the Boer War in South Africa, through Egypt and the First and Second World Wars, we get a sense of the reality of Empire in a port city, personalising and bringing to life events that can now seem so distant in time.

We also get the appearance of many Liverpool institutions and icons from Everton FC to Littlewoods Pools, from Dixie Dean to John Moores.

I won't spoil the tales and adventures of London life, including the darker side of the 60s and 70s but leave you to discover the love and tragedies for yourself, but look out for the man with a black Jaguar and dripping gold.

Brian recounts a personal family history that is wider than his own bloodline. The events and times they lived through are part of all our families' experiences. This is his family, but it could so easily be any of ours. In describing his parents experience of the blitz and watching bombs fall on Liverpool, we can relive the horror and danger of those times. In hearing of the refusal of governments then to accept Jews fleeing from Nazi persecution, we are reminded of current struggles of the ongoing forced displacement of the Palestinian people from their land.

Brian is proud to be a Mudman and a Scouser, and he has every right. Mudmen have indeed included some very famous names, many that Brian references in these pages, among them footballers and entertainers, but none more famous than Jack Jones, a renowned trade union leader, former leader of the Trades Union Congress (TUC), and later a fighter for pensioners' rights, who started life in Garston. Much less famous, but someone we should hold in no less esteem, is Brian's father, Denis Peter Mooney, who in the 1930s fought in the Spanish Civil War, alongside thousands of others from across the world in the International Brigades, to defend the Spanish Republic from Generalissimo Franco. Liverpool town hall has a plaque with the names of all the combatants from Liverpool who fought in that conflict, where Denis Mooney's name is proudly listed.

In highlighting his pride in his father's sacrifices to defend democracy in Spain, Brian is affirming the willingness to show solidarity with others that has always, and to this day remains one of the best traditions of the people of Liverpool.

I first saw the draft of this book many months ago and was convinced it would form a part of the social history of our city. Congratulations are due to Brian for writing and seeing this project through to publication, and to Writing On The Wall for supporting this venture. I wish it every success.

Jack Byrne

Author of Under The Bridge, Across The Water, and Before The Storm. His latest novel, Burning Down The House, is available from Northodox Press and all good bookshops.

Introduction

Due to a shrapnel wound in his leg, my dad was the only one of five brothers not to wear a British military uniform in World War II. His combat had taken place earlier on the arid plains and hills of Spain as a volunteer in The International Brigade. Little wonder then that the sons of Ex-Sergeant Major Denis Mooney J.P. were known to their Anfield neighbours as 'The Fighting Mooney's.' Two brothers would be wounded in Italy, one severely and sent home, the other treated near the scene of battle and returned to active service. Each of the Mooney boys survived, and all but one returned home to Liverpool. Due to tragic events in 1947, the once close brothers fragmented. Only my dad and his badly injured brother Desmond remained in their hometown.

The people whose blood I share are, I feel, more than worthy of remembrance. My parents gave me Liverpool roots with a background of sport, politics, the law, communications, and military action. I felt it important to write about such people, and the city that created them. It was also a chance to write of the 1950s childhood I spent 'under the bridge' in the dockland area of Garston, where a kid's playground was a bomb site (the 'bombies') or the woods, fields and muddy shore of the Mersey.

My writings began late in life, and, due to other commitments, occurred only spasmodically over a long period. I wrote much that was very honest and personal, and, for those reasons, I deliberately let the years go by until the characters named had passed on and I had a fuller picture of my own story.

Like tens of thousands before them, my ancestors arrived in Liverpool in search of a better life and opportunities. They came at a time when the seaport was second only in its importance to that of London. The Union Jack represented Queen Victoria's Empire and was proudly hoisted across the globe. British ships ruled the waves, and Liverpool's seven miles of docks overlooked a river that signified the strength of the world's most powerful nation. Ships of all types and sizes transported and imported people and goods across a globe of unparalleled movement. My forebears worked hard, integrated, and raised families. They became Liverpudlians in every sense. Some were well educated, some less so, but over the decades they would all contribute to the daily life of their city. They were people who faced whatever adversity beset them, never complained, but just rolled up their sleeves and got on with it.

My own small family unit remained in Liverpool until the mid-nineteen fifties, by which time its importance as a port had started to decline, mass unemployment lay just over the horizon, and the devastating effect of the 1941 bombings were still everywhere to be seen. Trying to raise three boys in very sub-standard housing conditions, and with no sign of improvement, my parents made the decision to move to London. They were not alone; tens of thousands of others enacted the same exodus. Though I was the youngest, I felt as my brothers did, that we were being robbed of who we were. We were children of the River Mersey. It's cold grey waves ran through our veins. We desperately did not want to leave behind everything we knew.

We never spoke out and just accepted that our parents knew best. However, on no occasion during the decades that followed did we ever allow ourselves to become Londoners. The 200 miles that lay between London and Liverpool were never an obstacle to us, and we returned at every given opportunity.

It may have been many decades ago, but I have remained a scouser, retaining a pride in knowing that I was a kid of that seaport during less privileged times. I am an old man now, but I still hold dear the good hearted, but gritty and tough people of my childhood. It was that hardiness I have tried to retain through good and unfavourable times.

TALES OF YORE

'I could write a book!' was one of our Auntie Maggie's favourite phrases. The odd thing was that she wasn't our auntie at all, but our grandmother. Such was her vanity and fear of old age that we never knew her by any other name. She had been widowed a year before wars end, had briefly remarried a Mr Troy, and had left him after only a few weeks describing him as a 'sex maniac!' She then moved constantly from one place to another in one room type accommodation around the Upper Parliament Street area. An international depression and a war had turned a once high market region of three-story Victorian houses into a deprived segment of humble flats and lodging rooms. Being on her own, it was hardly surprising that she would be a regular visitor to our Garston house.

Her words about writing a book normally led her into a tale or two of her life. We were supposedly in her care between school terms whilst our mam was at work. The only reason we were not outside playing was because of heavy rain. She would try her best to curtail the antics of three boisterous lads by saying, 'I spy with my little eye.' Temporarily she captured our attention, but after twenty minutes or so we had run out of objects to spy. It was then that she came out with little snippets of days gone by. Much to my later regret, and with my attention span being that of a seven-year-old, I only half listened.

It was only much later in life that I realised that Auntie Maggie's tales were important pieces of local history. They were anecdotes that explained the Liverpool of the past, and the characters from whom I derive. She would most certainly have had enough material from her life to write a book ,and looking back almost seventy years, perhaps it was her words that inspired me to do so.

A LATENT INTEREST IN THE PAST

I am the youngest of three brothers, aged eleven, nine and seven, and, as with most 1950s kids, our childhoods were without such luxuries as tv or the gadgets so predominant in today's world. Our entertainment came from playing in the street. Football in the winter, and cricket in the summer, intermingled with the odd game of kick-the-can. Those outdoor games, and the adventures we had down the Mersey shore was all we knew. It never bothered us, and we were happy in our ignorance.

As I grew, the pangs of youth, the lack of time, and later the commitment of family life, meant my interest in family history never amounted to much more than occasional reference talks with my older brothers. It was only after my dad's sudden death that I realised that none of us are immortal, and the past can, and often does, come back and slap us in the face. Alongside that terrible shock came the realisation that there was so much I did not know about him. It was not just him however, it was everything regarding my whole family on both my parents' sides. The idea of researching and recording my family's past, intermingled with my own memories became important to me. As soon as it was possible I would document whatever information I could gather.

As with much of Liverpool, poor housing had put a large portion of Garston on the demolition list of the city's planners. The destruction began slowly in the late 1950s and early 1960s, and bit by bit during the following decades Garston had its heart ripped out. Many families were scattered to the city's outer regions or beyond, the factories closed, and the docker's hook became a relic of the past. City planner's final act of eradicating Garston's 'under the bridge' was the opening of a by-pass that cut out whatever reasons there had once been to stop. Shops, pubs, the swimming baths, and the cinemas all ceased to be, and the Garston I knew was gone in all but name.

CELTIC STOCK WITH A DASH OF YORKSHIRE

When I began my research, it did not take long for me to discover that I came from people who had made their mark. Through all the turbulence of the 19th and 20th century, they retained an optimism and sense of tenacity. They had brought with them a predominantly Celtic and gritty northern outlook, and they blended in well with their fellow immigrant neighbours. During that 19th century period, Liverpool people were evolving. Though in Lancashire, the port was different to its county neighbours. This was because Liverpool was a port, and therefore people of different creeds and religions influenced each other. Predominantly Irish and Welsh, there were also many Scots, African, West Indian, and Chinese. The Liverpudlian developed into a new breed of northerner, who due to the introduction by Norwegian whalers of a cheaply made stew, became known as scousers. A DNA test showed my blood to be Irish, Welsh and Scottish with a dash of Yorkshire.

THE WINTER OF DISCONTENT –
SNOW, RUBBISH, AND LOSS

LONDON 1979

The last year of the 1970s began horrendously for the people of London. By February heavy snow carpeted the capital, made far worse by the strikes of firemen, grave diggers, ambulance drivers, and refuse workers. Thousands of unemptied dustbins and rubbish bags were piled high on the pavements of almost every street. My parents lived in Archway, North London, close to Hampstead Heath and Parliament Hill Fields, so foxes became a common sight as they roamed the streets feasting on man's garbage. They were joined, though less visibly, by an increase in the rat population.

Rain or snow, my parents still worked, even though both had officially retired. My mam had continued freelance waitressing, something she had done as well as a daytime job at John Lewis in Oxford Street. Such jobs took her inside another world. Her most prestigious event in the calendar year was at the Queen's garden party every summer. In actual fact, she was presented to the Queen on two occasions. Being a Royalist, it was something she was very proud of. Other events she looked forward to were the Ascot races, and the Lord Mayor's Annual Show. She would come back and tell us who were the tippers, and who weren't. My dad, being good at figures, got himself a job in a bookies. Not being allowed to bet on the premises must have been hard, as he loved his gee gees.

My concern for them grew as the snow made conditions in London far worse. I watched the gloom unfold nightly on the news from the comfort of my home in Jersey. I went to bed on one of those cold February nights not realising that within hours I would be entering one of the darkest periods of my life.

'Is that Mr Mooney, Mr Brian Mooney,' a woman's voice asked?

I was still half asleep but awake enough to realise that a telephone call at three in the morning could only be bad news. She asked if I was sitting down and explained that she was a policewoman and was phoning on behalf of my mother. My dad had been rushed to Whittington Hospital having suffered a heart attack.

'Your mother is with him, and the doctors are very concerned. He is very poorly Mr Mooney, and if it's at all possible we suggest you try to get to London as soon as you can.' Those carefully phrased words made me realise that my dad's time on earth was limited. Fighting back the tears I thanked her, and as quietly as I could I returned to my bed, grateful that my two young children hadn't been woken. My late wife June consoled me until my tears eventually turned into a half sleep.

Early the next morning I awoke to an island that was shrouded not in snow, but in fog! Fog in Jersey means only one thing, the closing of the airport! So, there I was, desperate to say my goodbyes, but unable to do so. No planes arrived or flew out that day and it was another thirty-six hours before my feet walked across the tarmac of Heathrow Airport. It was miserable, I was cold, my eyes were damp, and my heart was heavy. Earlier that day I learned that I was too late, my dad had died. One thing my mother told me still touches my heart over forty years later. Though very weak, when he learnt I was flying over, my dad asked my mam for a comb and his false teeth. There was one lesson I learned that day, and that is how we take people for granted, not adequately showing them how important they are until it's too late. Liked by all who knew him, my dad was an honest and decent gentleman with strong convictions.

Though none of my family had lived in Liverpool for nearly a quarter of a century, my dad's death threw me back to the childhood man we nicknamed 'Father Fleck.' Quite why he acquired that nickname I still don't know. He was the interesting unassuming man who educated us in so many little ways. The good father who taught us cards games, and who took his family out each Sunday to broaden their horizons. The dad who in later years could be relied upon to do the little things in life, like bringing home the fish and chips each Friday night on his way home from work. The loss of my dad took my mind back a quarter of a century to a little Garston dockside street.

THE MAN IN THE BLACK JAGUAR

AUGUST 1955

Peeking through their netted curtains, several Shand Street women just couldn't contain their curiosity. The second world war had ended a decade before, but times were still difficult, and for certain nobody in Shand Street, or the surrounding streets owned a car. Yet pulling up outside number thirty-four on that warm summer's morning of 1955 was a large black 1939 Jaguar. Cloth capped men on their way to the docks or nearby factories were taken aback, not only by the grandness of the vehicle, but also by the trilby hatted and expensively suited man who emerged from it onto the pavement. The man in question was making a call that would change the lives of my family forever.

Not yet nine years old, I was still in bed. Getting up for school was temporarily off the agenda, and I lay there thinking of the coming summer of adventure. In my comatose state I was picturing days spent playing in the fields, ponds, and woods that awaited alongside the nearby muddy shores of the Mersey. Though semi-conscious, I had the whole bedroom to myself, with both my elder brothers having risen and gone downstairs. Through bleary eyes I could see the sun gleaming through the makeshift nylon curtains that had once been my uncle George's wartime parachute.

Though drowsy, I became aware of my parents talking in the kitchen to a male voice that I didn't recognise. Gradually, curiosity got the better of me, and I dragged myself from my slumbers and made my way down the bare wooden staircase. To an eight-year-old boy, the figure I beheld looked like he had stepped out of the silver screen. Younger and broader than my dad, he was not yet into middle age and was unlike any man I had ever come into close contact with. He had removed his trilby and jacket, and on the breast pocket of his white silk shirt were the hand stitched initials B.M.

'This is your uncle Bryan,' my mam said.

I was too shy to reply but couldn't take my eyes off the huge gold ring on his finger and the thick gold bracelet on his wrist. I just stood there in awe, trying to process the fact that this handsomely groomed character was my dad's brother. Not able to fully understand what was going on, I took a step back, anxious just to listen to my elders. I studied the features of my new uncle. It was obvious that he was a Mooney, but his character was very different to that of my dad. He had an obvious swagger, a definite self-assurance, and a slight London accent. He also had all the trappings of someone who was at ease with himself and enjoyed the trappings of money. The unlawful way he acquired that money we were yet to find out. Such facts would only be divulged gradually in the months that followed, by which time it was all too late.

As the grown-ups talked, I began to remember the recent mention of one of my dad's younger brothers living in London, and that it had been many years since he had been in contact. I later learned that on his way to work several weeks before, my dad had seen a council road sweeper who he recognised as being a friend of my uncle from before the war. My dad was in no doubt, as the man in question was a big burly black West Indian, and a musical pal of Uncle Bryan. Never one to hold any racist feelings, my dad approached him with the question "Do you know Bryan Mooney?" Not only was the answer affirmative, but he informed my dad that he had Bryan's London address. The two men arranged to meet the next morning, and twenty-four hours later my dad was duly furnished with his long-lost brother's place of residence. During the next few weeks letters went back and forth between the brothers, climaxing with my uncle's visit.

The conversation in our tiny kitchen seemed to be about how well my uncle was doing, he said he had properties, and that we should all move to London and rent one of his flats. I knew that my parents had their names down for rehousing, but I was also aware that the council lists were very long, and that in all probability our chances of a council house in the near future were very slim. Living in an area known as 'under the bridge', the housing was near to the docks and industry and was listed for demolition. So too was much of Liverpool, and Garston residents were in ignorance as to when such demolitions would occur (records show that in 1963 only 10% of the Garston houses listed in the 1950s for demolition had been removed).

Whilst we three brothers were more than happy with our little house, our parents quite rightly wanted better for their boys. The talk continued about a move to London. Being just a kid, I was totally unaware that Liverpool's population was decreasing rapidly, and its prospects were seen as grim. I listened intently as the discussion progressed about London, and how it would be a place of opportunity for us boys. Laced in the conversation was my uncle's bragging of how he had fallen on his feet. He unfortunately remained tight-lipped and evasive as to how he had earned his assets. He was always vague and would remain so throughout the decades that followed. He was a mystery man, an enigma, only ever telling you what he wanted you to know.

As the conversation continued, it became obvious that we were London bound. We three brothers never gave an opinion, nor were we asked for one. To us, our parents always knew best. That doesn't mean that we were happy with the prospect of leaving. We loved Garston with its mixture of industry and shoreline. We were baby boom kids who knew the joy of playing in the streets or down by the banks of the Mersey. Kids who grasped and appreciated the changing seasons of nature that the shore gave us. Street kids who loved the gas lamp posts we had converted into swings, and the chalk marked pavements where girls played hopscotch, and twirled ropes while skipping to old traditional rhymes. Boys who converted old prams into racing chariots. Young lads who weren't afraid of getting dirty, and who enjoyed a freedom without adult interference. Kids who knew the joy of play, and who went home only when they had to.

LONDON BOUND - NO TURNING BACK

It had been decided. We were going to leave our whole way of life and travel two hundred miles to a place we knew nothing of. We were doing so on the word of a man who had suddenly reappeared after a decade long absence. A man who said much, but in fact said little. The next few weeks were a terrible strain on my mam. My dad had gone on ahead to London to find work, and she had the unenviable task of selling off as much as she could of our household goods, informing our schools, and tying up all the loose ends. The one thing I particularly remember was people coming into the house and buying our books for pennies. My mam needed every cent she could lay her hands on, and every penny counted. The hardest thing she had to do was to inform the lady we knew as our Auntie Maggie. Our mam knew that her mother would not take our leaving Liverpool lightly, and she was right. Everything was a drama with Auntie Maggie, and this news was no exception. She took it very badly. My mams younger sister Joan was more realistic and supportive, seeing it as an opportunity.

The day of our departure was one that I shall never forget and added greatly to the respect I held for Garstonians. Auntie Maggie sat weeping on the stairs with her head in her hands. This didn't lighten my mams' already heavy burden. I had never been in a taxi before, but the added expense was because we had so much to carry. Our sadness was lightened slightly by the sight of our neighbours. All the way up our little street and beyond people stood at their doorways to say goodbye. Such scenes of genuine kindness remain with me almost seventy years later. I made an inner oath that I would never lose contact with my city or its wonderful people. Thankfully, this is an oath I have been able to keep. Wherever I have travelled, I have proudly boasted that I am a scouser. Even in the London schools where I was belittled about my accent, I continued to say **'bath** not *barth,'* and '**grass** not *grarse.'* It got me into numerous fights, but I retained my scouse accent.

When I set out to write, I deliberately focused on those who arrived in Liverpool when a map of the world was covered in the pink of Victorian Britain. Those were the ones I felt more of an affinity to. The ones who honoured me by making Liverpool my birthplace. So, who were they? Well, with the aid of a Liverpool Echo segment called 'Liverpool Pals,' Liverpool Central Library, much computer investigation, my own memories, and with help from my family and friends, a journey into my Liverpool roots began.

THE SEEDS FROM WHENCE I CAME

PATERNAL ROOTS: DENIS PETER MOONEY (1854-1909)

My great grandfather Denis Peter Mooney was born just after Southern Ireland had lost one million of its people to the Potato Famine. His first breath was taken in Dalkey, an affluent coastal town southeast of Dublin. The seaside town, with its very pretty harbour, is today described as The Beverley Hills of Dublin, due to it being a chosen residence of pop stars (Bono and Van Morrison) and a Hollywood actor (Matt Damon).

In the 19th century it would have been a tranquil area for middle class Dubliners to escape to. With seals in its harbour, one source of the village's income would have been fishing, another would have been its supply of granite. There was a large quarry which the Mooney family had an involvement with. Today, the remains of that quarry make it a popular place for rock climbers. Denis Peter would appear to have been born into reasonably comfortable circumstances. He was a Protestant, but how or when his family converted from Catholicism, I have no idea. Being Protestant would certainly have helped sustain a position of privilege in a country that was castigated by its British rulers because of its Catholic beliefs.

Denis Peter was the son of Laurence and Ellen Mooney. Laurence must have been a man with means as there is a legal document of him renting a three-story Georgian house in the prestigious Granby Row properties of Dublin in the late 1850's. Young Denis Peter received a good education which led to him becoming a telegrapher for the American company Western Union in their Dublin office. The family had moved earlier to Meath, north of the city. Married in the early 1870s, Denis Peter transferred to Liverpool. I presume that he had requested the transfer as there was a family connection through his wife, my great grandmother (Ellen Molloy 1858-1893). There was an army connection also, which I am only able to speculate on, a little later. Denis Peter was in his late 20's, at this time, and a family photo shows him to be quite a dapper fellow. He is pictured in 1883 alongside his fellow Western Union staff in front of the magnificent Exchange Flags Building, a beautiful structure whose piazza styled frontage was used by cotton traders. That piazza is still there, the old building having been replaced in 1939. In the group photo his fellow office staff look sombre in their dark Victorian draped outfits, but Denis Peter is suited dandily in light grey. He was described on one 19th century census as an electrician. On another, his job title is telegrapher. It's possible that he was both or switched from one to the other. To be an electrician and a telegrapher would certainly have made him an asset to America's largest telecommunications company. One thing is for sure, he was a dedicated employee and spent his whole working life with the company.

As stated, there is some confusion regarding my great grandfather's army involvement. I found some information on him in his son's obituary. Printed in April 1958, the Liverpool Echo stated that Denis Peter had served in the King's Liverpool Irish Regiment Volunteer Brigade as a Comp Sgt Major. This is a mystery to me, but I have concluded that he had joined the army at a very young age, served for a few years, then retained his association in a unit similar to today's territorial army. The article seems to show that he knew Liverpool well before his permanent move from Dublin. I have no proof as to the true facts, however, so it is pure conjecture. Crossing the Irish Sea meant Denis Peter had to leave his young family behind whilst he settled into his job and set about finding adequate accommodation. They eventually joined him, and the family made their permanent home in Anfield.

SOLDIER, SPORTSMAN, AND JUSTICE OF THE PEACE
DENIS MOONEY (1881-1958)

Eight years younger than his sister Georgina, my

grandfather Denis arrived in Liverpool as a very young child. I know nothing of his early years, but I am certain he went to the very prestigious Liverpool Collegiate College. He was a boy with an interested and active mind, coupled with a great physical ability for sport. Aged twelve, his first taste of tragedy struck when his mother Ellen died. Making matters worse for him, was his father's quick remarriage two years later, and the arrival of two step-siblings. Being at an awkward age, it must have been an unsettling time for a young lad, but he was active, and his surroundings gave him much to occupy his mind.

The Liverpool of the 1890s would have been exciting times for a young lad brought up in a comfortable Anfield home. Sport was a definite interest, at a time when Liverpool and the whole of the northwest had become gripped by football. The opening of the nearby Goodison Park Stadium when Denis was 11 years old ensured that he would remain a true Evertonian all his life. Denis would have taken great pride in so many unique aspects of Liverpool. One of which would have been the opening of the world's first electrically operated overhead railway in 1893. Running from Dingle to Seaforth, this magnificent construction allowed its passengers to view the whole length of the Liverpool dock system, giving views of hundreds of ships of all classes from the four corners of the world.

There can be little doubt that young Denis would have joined the thousands of others who paid their fare to view the magnificence of such a sight. Being a reader, Denis probably knew that Charles Dickens once said, 'Liverpool lies in my heart, second only to London.' Mr Dickens was a frequent visitor to the city, his choice of accommodation was always the first Adelphi Hotel, of which there have been three.

As he grew, my grandfather learned to appreciate the greatness of his surroundings. For those with an education and a good job it was a glorious age, and the town centre reflected that period with its beautiful buildings. Denis was a young man with an enquiring mind, and he took in every aspect and piece of information he could. He would have marvelled at the amazing architecture that was well in keeping with Liverpool being a major port of the Empire. He would have been proud that Queen Victoria described St Georges Hall as being 'Worthy of ancient Athens.' He may even have been aware that the beautiful structure was the first of its kind to have an air conditioning system. Britain's most noted late 19th century architect Richard Norman Shaw put it best by quite simply declaring the hall to be 'The finest building in Europe.' An exaggeration possibly, but it remains an eye-catching, and very grand structure. Perhaps my grandfather was even aware that near to his father's place of work, stood The Oriel Buildings, which were constructed with a totally new architectural concept. Steel framed blocks allowed huge windows to cover the whole of the front facade. The idea was 'borrowed' by American architects, and the results were the New York skyscrapers!

The spectacle of Liverpool's docks would have stirred the imagination of a young man like Denis. American novelist Herman Melville (author of Moby Dick) described the wondrous scene by writing, 'In Liverpool I beheld long China walls of masonry; vast piers of stone; and a succession of granite rimmed docks, completely enclosed. The extent and solidity of these structures seemed equal to what I had read of the old pyramids of Egypt. The docks of Liverpool, even at this present day, surpass all others in the world.'

As was normal for the time, Denis had followed in his father's footsteps and joined his place of employment. Beginning at the bottom as a messenger, Denis Mooney was to rise into management for the prestigious American Company. As mentioned, his father had remarried and started a new family. Unsurprisingly, it would have been an emotional and difficult time for young Denis, especially as his older sister Georgina had also married and left the family home.

Denis had enjoyed his education and became an avid

reader. He lost himself in tales of adventure and far off lands. He would have been aware of the term used by novelist Jack London 'Go west young man.' The gold rush of Alaska had captured the imagination of every young reader. My grandfather would have been sixteen at the time, and he daydreamed of heading west in search of his fortune. Finances, and his young age put paid to such thoughts, but he retained a longing for travel, excitement, and perhaps the thrill of danger.

The only way for a young dreamer like Denis to satisfy his restless spirits was to join the British Army. Conveniently, the Boer colonists in South Africa (who had derived from Dutch, German, and French Protestant farmers) had taken up arms to resist encroachment into land they had developed independently in the region. Though other reasons were given, of course the main reason for the outbreak of war was land, as it always is. The British were still expansionists, and South Africa was rich in diamonds and gold. The Boer farmers were opposed to British interference and were willing to fight for land they considered to be theirs. The dispute had been going on for twenty years leading to the major confrontation that broke out in 1899.

The Boers were excellent horsemen, knew their terrain, and most were crack riflemen and were well armed with the very prestigious Howitzer rifles. They were also unconventional fighters, who used the hit and run tactics of the guerilla. They were achieving great successes and the British public, spurred on by the media, demanded that the matter be concluded once and for all. From late 1900, British General Herbert Kitchener was placed in charge. His methods were ruthless. Farms and crops were destroyed, livestock rounded up or killed, and dissenters arbitrarily executed. Detention camps were already in use, but Kitchener extended their use by placing nearly 150,000 men, women and children behind barbed wire in what were the world's first concentration camps. There were 45 such detention prisons, and the crowded and unsanitary conditions were appalling. As well as fatalities from a measles epidemic, the lack of food and water led to 25,000 Boer deaths. How much of all this my grandfather knew of or participated in I do not know, and perhaps that is for the best. I will put it into the context that he was a soldier, and asked no questions, but obeyed orders, and had been instilled, as most young men were at the time, with a deep sense of service to Queen and Country.

The army was the perfect way for a young man like Denis to find the adventure he craved. I know little of his time in South Africa, other than he had found his niche in soldiering. He had enlisted aged eighteen and by his 20th birthday had risen to become a Sergeant

Major, one of the youngest men ever to do so. Army life, the thrill of battle, and the comradeship of men was the start of a life of leadership and commitment for Denis Mooney.

With the Boers crushed into submission, he returned to civilian life late in 1902, his job at Western Union having been kept open. The army, the travel, and the adventure were however still transfixed into his very being. So much so that his spare time was spent with local peacetime army units. Given his own troop, he later enlisted in The Pembrokeshire Yeomanry who were based in Penally, Tenby in South Wales. This meant that in the event of his services being needed again, he would be ready. Obviously, he retained his rank, and any spare time he got, he would leave Liverpool and catch a train to South Wales.

Margaret Sarah Davies married ex Company Sgt Denis Mooney in 1908, the same year as the death of his father Denis Peter. Margaret was a factory worker at Ogden's Imperial Tobacco Company in Everton, a beautiful building that had been opened for business in 1901. Born in 1884, Margaret's family had arrived in the 1870s from Leigh in Lancashire. The Davie tree shows them originating from just outside Edinburgh, having spent time in Cumberland. It is said that Margaret was employed as a maker of special hand rolled cigarettes, and that such was her dexterity that she had once been sent by the company to a new factory in Bristol to train selected women in the art.

One major problem with the marriage was religion, as was often the case in Liverpool. Denis was a Protestant, and Margaret Sarah had been raised in the Roman Catholic Church. Normally, the man would give up his doctrine, but not in the case of my grandparents. I do not know where the marriage took place, or of any family problems the union would have created. What I am certain of is that Denis had no time for religion and would have been vehemently opposed to the rulings and doctrinations of Rome!

Being prepared for war, the riding of horses, and the leadership of men remained important to my grandfather. As stated earlier, he visited and went on exercises as often as he could in Tenby with his yeomanry troop. His opportunity for more adventure came along not in 1914 in The Great War against Germany, but a year later when the enemy was Turkey. Horse units with skills in providing communication were needed in the middle east. As well as extending the Ottoman territories, and aided by Germany, the Turks were trying to take control of the Suez Canal, a construction of vital importance to both the British and the French. Whoever controlled the canal, controlled the far east. The men of the Royal Engineers 75th Signal Corps, under the command of Troop Sgt Major Denis

Mooney found themselves despatched by ship to Egypt. The war would be long and protracted, for the Turks were a formidable enemy who had enjoyed great successes. The hot terrain made it difficult enough for European troops, but it was made far, far worse because of inadequate water supplies. The unit were responsible for laying cables and ensuring that communications were in place for the different army units. With his expertise regarding radio and communications, my grandfather was in his element. The troop would also have been adept in picking up and relaying the messages of the enemy. It is unimaginable to think how uncomfortable this would have been under such in unforgiving sun and nights of terrible cold. 170,000 Egyptian volunteers transported water with the assistance of 72,500 camels.

Under his leadership, my grandfather's unit was so successful in their work that Sgt Major Denis Mooney was Mentioned in Despatches (MiD) for gallantry by General Sir Edmund Allenby, the leader of the Egyptian Expeditionary Force. A personal letter of thanks from King George V and the Minister of War Winston Churchill was sent to my grandfather in 1919 after the war had ended in victory and is still in my possession. After being demobbed, my grandfather entered another and very personal period of his life. The guns may have been silenced, but Denis Mooney was not ready to sit back and accept a life of reflective domesticity.

On his return to civilian life, Denis was once again able to pick up where he had left off with Western Union. He was now to take up the mantle of life as father to a growing family. Big families were the order of the day, and Denis and Margaret Sarah seemed a very devoted couple, as they produced six children, five boys and one girl. He loved working for Western Union and climbed the ladder into a position which held the rather mysterious and title of 'Special Agent'. His duties included welcoming and representing his company to V.I.P. Americans. Family tales say that one of the big-name Americans he met was Buffalo Bill, when the showman brought his Wild West Show to Liverpool.

Though his war had been fighting Turks in North Africa, he was aware of the horrors endured by those lucky enough to have returned from France. Walking the streets of his city, he bore witness to hundreds of post war jobless young men, idly standing on street corners. He felt a great affinity with those lost souls, most of whom were ex-soldiers who had been amongst the unparalleled slaughter of the trenches. They had fought bravely, seen their comrades die, and been promised a land fit for heroes. There was no such thing as counselling, and unemployment, poor wages and a lack of self-worth brought about a deeply felt discontent. Denis Mooney could not help but be moved by the plight of such men, and was determined to do what he could through politics. He threw all his energy into everything he ever did, and that attitude saw him campaigning and supporting The Liberal Party.

Having been born a proud Irishman, he was aware that it was the Liberals, under the leadership of Prime Minister William Gladstone, who had tried and failed on two occasions to get Parliament to give Ireland Home Rule. My grandfather would have approved, but I cannot see him wishing to see Ireland as a totally independent republic, but rather an independent State within The United Kingdom. He took the King's shilling because it gave him the adventure he craved, and wore an English soldier's uniform, but he always remained a child of Ireland.

Due to its staunch Catholicism and devotion to Rome, England's treatment of the Irish had been shameful for centuries, The Liberal Party's attempts to help Ireland would have been admired by Denis Mooney. He joined the party, and as with everything else in his life, he did so with enthusiasm and vigour. As a result of such commitment, he was eventually voted in as the Chairman of The West Derby Branch.

Photos show him to have been like his father, a very dapper and well-dressed man about town. Never one to stand back and accept the situation, but unable to provide those unfortunate men with jobs, he found another solution to make their lives a little better, and that was through sport! Having always been active, and particularly with his sons, he encouraged unemployed men away from the street corners and up to Stanley Park to partake in cricket, football and American baseball.

It was during the 1920s that baseball had gained in popularity in the north and midlands. Leagues had been formed, and two friends who both worked in The Exchange Flags building cooperated with each other and created Everton Baseball Club. The friend in question was named John Moores, who would become one of England's richest entrepreneurs. The two men worked for different telegraphy companies, but both were stationed within the pre 1939 Exchange Flags Building off Dale Street.

Primarily a telegrapher, John Moores was the kind of man one would best describe as being a 'go-getter.' He had a sideline within the massive building as a bookies runner. Betting on horses outside of the racecourse was illegal until the1960s with the opening of betting shops, hence the bookies runner! In every area, and in every town and city, one could find a bookies runner. He was the man who you could place an illegal bet with.

It may have been outside of the law, but where there is a need, there is a way! John Moores was a man with drive, and a man who was going places. Exchange Flags had many company offices, and I would imagine many of the employees enjoyed a flutter. That being the case, John Moores was the man to see. Strangely, he had become friendly with my grandfather, a none betting man.

John Moores, telegrapher and bookies runner, was a man out to make his fortune. The idea of a 'football pool' was first devised by John Jervis, a Birmingham man, but he had struggled to make a profit. John Moores was convinced that the idea could be improved, and in 1923 he and three friends launched Littlewood Football Pools. Two years later the 'Pool' was still running at a loss, and Moores' partners bailed out. That left Moores in sole control, and within five years he was a millionaire. The interesting thing, however, was that in those early days of struggle Moores had approached my grandfather for financial help and a stake in the business. Well, my grandfather never became a millionaire, but the two men did remain friends. My Uncle Bryan would tell me of the envious neighbours who would ogle at the white Rolls Royce that was often parked outside the Anfield home of Denis Mooney in the late twenties and early 1930s. John Moores was not a native Liverpudlian but had originated from just outside Manchester. Possibly because they both worked for American companies, baseball became a passion for both men, and using John Moore's obvious financial attributes they aided each other, along with other enthusiasts to create a Liverpool league. The two men also shared a love of Everton Football Club, and with baseball being a summer sport, Everton players were recruited into the newly formed Everton Baseball Club. One of those players was the legendary Dixie Dean, the man who still holds the record of most scored goals (60), in the season of 1927/28.

My grandfather had remained committed to getting the unemployed involved in sport throughout the 1920's and into the 1930's. In 1936 his services were recognised, and he was rewarded by the City of Liverpool, when he was offered, and accepted, the position of **Justice of the Peace**. It was perfect timing, as that was the year that he retired from Western Union. Sport and politics, and a large family of sports minded boys had more than kept his adventurous spirit active, and now he must have felt an inner satisfaction to be rewarded by his city. I do recall hearing that he often had problems with some of his fellow J.P.s who would try to interfere with his decisions, presuming him to be a fellow Freemason. My grandfather got to his position due to his endeavours to get the unemployed involved in sport, and not by any devious funny handshakes. When favours were asked, he gave them short shrift. My own memories of my grandfather, which are few and far between, are of a stern upright old man who, surrounded by cats, stood with his back to his fireplace like the sergeant major he had once been. He would rise up and down on his toes as if he was inspecting his troops. There was no warmth towards his grandsons, just a coldness and superiority. I do recall him once placing a threepenny 'joey' on the table and saying to my mam, 'this is for the boys' – she did not pick it up. At the time I didn't understand why, but age has taught me that my mam was quite a gal. I learned many years later that he thought his eldest son had married beneath him. No such behaviour was ever reciprocated by my grandmother, who showed my mam nothing but kindness. I suppose Denis Mooney was a product of his time. A typical Edwardian with a 'stiff upper lip'. My mam wasn't going to give him the satisfaction of making him feel good about himself with threepence placed on a table, instead of giving them one ounce of affection. I'm sure that threepenny piece was given in kindness, but the lack of emotion was something that wrangled my very blunt mother. I shall return to my grandfather and what happened to him later.

HOMEMAKER. GOOD WIFE. GOOD MOTHER. MARGARET SARAH DAVIE (1883-1947)

I do not remember my paternal grandmother, but I would like to think she had held me in her arms. I was a just a seven-month-old baby when she died in 1947.

Her death was due to 'takotsubo cardiomyopathy' brought about by a surge of stress hormones due to an emotionally stressful event. To put that in layman's terms, it means she died of a broken heart. The traumatic event was the death of her 23-year-old daughter three months before. I have much to say about these tragic events because they play an important part in my family story. Therefore, I leave them temporarily to a later and larger section.

My grandmother was born in Liverpool, her parents having moved some time earlier from just outside Manchester. In research, I found her forebears had originally come from Cumberland and Edinburgh, Scotland. Margaret Sarah had been raised in the Catholic Church, but married Protestant Denis Mooney in 1908. Just what difficulties this led to I don't know, but I would imagine it was not welcomed by families on either side. Strangely enough, my Great Grandfather died the same year.

There were many such mixed religion marriages in Liverpool, and they often led to the breakup of families. It would have been out of the norm if Denis or Margaret Sarah had not been met by some kind of opposition. The problem certainly showed its face on the birth of my father their first child. Whilst my grandfather was away for his Yeomanry duties in South Wales, my grandmother and her sister had my dad Christened by a Roman Catholic priest. Probably thinking that her child would be burnt in hell as a heretic, the two colluded to baptise my dad in secret. I do not know how Denis Mooney handled the news on his return. All I do know is that my dad never entered a Catholic church again, and none of his siblings were given the same start in life. I do not know if Margaret Sarah Mooney ever led her own private Catholic life, but I have grave doubts. In fact, after my dad's secretive Christening, I would think that the tricky subject of religion never raised its head in 12 Finchley Road again.

There is not much known about my grandmother's life other than she was a diligent and loving wife and mother. Due to Denis's liking for order, I think that the household was run like a well-oiled ship, which would have become obvious upon entering the front door with the children's shoes and coats all neatly placed in a line in accordance to age. Denis would have been a good but stiff-necked father who was the master of the house. Margaret Sarah would have been the kind of mother who was soft hearted and often turned a blind eye to what her five boys got up to. The kind of mother who baked cakes and was responsible for running a happy home. I would think she felt she had married a driven man, and that her job was to be dutiful and to simplify his life. I cover the tragedy of my grandmothers in a later chapter.

THE VOLUNTEER FIGHTER FOR SPAIN
DENIS PETER MOONEY (1909-1979)

Born one year after his parents' marriage; my dad was named after his grandfather who had died the year before. He would be followed by four brothers and a sister. When he was six, he lost the influence of a father figure as his dad was in the Middle East fighting the Turks. It must have been a very difficult time for his mother, but I think she understood if there was a war, her husband would be involved. Shortly after his father's return to civilian life, my dad was enrolled into Liverpool Collegiate College. The education was renowned for being of the highest of standards and some of the teachers had come to teach from Oxford. My dad would most certainly have been a good student, because all his life he was a man with a perfect head for maths, and an equal talent for English. He did have one drawback at the college however, he was left-handed.

I have read that such schools did not allow students to write with any hand other than the one on the right. Apparently, some such schools would even tie the left hand up behind the pupils back during English lessons. Well, whatever they did to my dad, it paid off for he became ambidextrous, meaning he could write with both left and right hand with dexterity. Not only that, but he had achieved the amazing skill of using two pens, one in each hand, and writing his name simultaneously with handwriting perfection from both hands. The college also gave my dad a great love of sport, and a special talent for cricket. On leaving school, he followed the normal pattern of many and joined his father into Western Union. He started at the bottom, as his father had done, as a messenger.

My dad had already been introduced to stamp collecting by his father, and Liverpool was probably one of the best places in England to build up a collection. Over the course of a day he went into countless offices of international companies where he would politely request that the staff he met save the stamps from the worldwide mail they received. He built up a global collection that was truly amazing, many from colonial countries that later changed their names.

I know virtually nothing of his teenage years. Being handsome, well-groomed, and polite, I would presume he was popular with the opposite sex. At some stage in the early 1930s he was transferred to the Edinburgh office, but how long he was there is lost in time. He certainly became fond of Scotland's fortress city and often spoke of it in later years. This would have been at the time of the great worldwide depression. By the early 1930s my dad was back in Liverpool and unemployed. The reason for his return is another great mystery. It is possible that he was made redundant as were so many others. I simply do not know, but for the first time in his life he was unemployed. Hardly surprising then that he became interested in politics. To understand how defining the next several years were for my dad, it is worth explaining what a terrible time the 1930s were for the world. It was a period of terrible recession and mass unemployment for millions worldwide. Governments searched for solutions, and Fascist dictators took advantage, gained power, and used extreme and deadly methods on those who stood in their way. Military tactics increased in civilian life and suddenly uniformed units appeared everywhere. It soon became obvious that world peace was a temporary luxury. Britain, along with France, because of the loss of so many young men twenty years before, chose the road of appeasement and non-interference. Their indifference was the catalyst to my dad's new interest in politics.

A would-be dictator had sprung up in Britain also, offering easy and quick Nationalistic solutions. His name was Sir Oswald Mosley, an aristocrat ex M.P. He had witnessed Fascism in Italy and Germany, been overly impressed, and with financial backing from influential aristocrats and business friends, he set up his own neo-Nazi Party. Dressed in intimidating dark military uniforms and jackboots, his group of British

Fascists became known as the Black Shirts. Everything about the party was in line with the image of the Fascists of Germany and Italy. The way they marched and strutted, their flag waving rallies, and the finger pointing and arm waving speeches of their leaders. As with Hitler, Mosley pointed all the problems at the feet of the Jews. He even organised a rally to march through Cable Street in the Jewish East London area. Of course, riots and violence prevailed, but that was always Mosley's plan. A year later he organised a rally in Queens Drive Liverpool to address a gathering of 8,000. Unfortunately, Mr Mosley never got the chance to air his views, for no sooner had he stood on top of a van to deliver his oratory, than he was made semi-conscious by a well-aimed brick. Hundreds more such missiles were thrown by the angry crowd before horsed police officers forced them back. Mosley was rushed to Walton Hospital where he spent the next week recuperating. Not surprisingly, he never returned to Liverpool again. Had Denis Mooney been in Liverpool on that day, there is no doubt in my mind that he would have been at that meeting. However, his way of showing his distaste for fascists was fighting them with a rifle thousands of miles away in The Spanish Civil War!

It was obvious to everyone in 1937 that the threat of another great war was looming. Hitler, in violation of all the treaties signed by Germany after their defeat in World War 1, had built up the army, navy, and Airforce. German children were being indoctrinated into the belief that they were the Master Race, and that the Jews and Slavic peoples were subhuman. Newly opened Dachau Concentration Camp was full of those considered enemies of the State. Homosexuals, gypsies, Marxists, priests, and anyone who spoke up or questioned the regime were rounded up and imprisoned. Their lives were made into a daily endurance of hard manual labour, brutality, and even murder. All books that The Nazis decided were against the new ideology, were banned or burnt. Freedom of thought had become virtually illegal, and every aspect of German life was now Nazified. Introduced in 1933, the 'Nuremberg Laws' curtailed most rights German Jews had. All these facts were known, yet Britain and France followed a policy of non-intervention. Such happenings were abhorrent to any clear minded thinker. To many, fascism had been allowed to get out of control. Similar human rights were being openly erased elsewhere in Europe.

In Italy, Benito Mussolini, with the full backing of the Vatican, had become 'Il Duce' (the duke, or the leader) of Italy in 1922. He introduced laws banning all opposition, newspapers, public protest meetings, and all political opponents to his Fascist Party. Unions were disbanded, all strikes were made illegal, and a new political secret police force was introduced. In 1935, while the world watched, his forces had invaded and occupied Abyssinia. His long-term plans were to do the same with other countries in North Africa and the Adriatic region.

Such dangers to democracy and world peace occurred with no intervention from Europe's two largest powers. Seen as a weakness by both Hitler and Mussolini, both continued to expand their draconian rules as the world stood idly by.

My dad was the first son of Denis Mooney to go to war. The Spain of the 1930s was similar in its order to the Spain of 100 years before, and 100 years before that! Small tenant farmers, mostly uneducated, eked out basic and meagre livings on small parcels of land owned by wealthy landowners. That is how it had remained over the centuries. Basically, country people were treated as peasants, and life was cruel, hard, and with little hope for improvement. Some particularly dry and poor crop years meant starvation and death. This suited the ultra-Conservative Catholic Church of Spain, who had a reputation for preferring to keep the churches full, and the minds of the peasants in unquestioning obedience. Such obedience also benefitted industrialists, and an army that was top heavy with over indulged generals.

An election had taken place where socialists had been democratically elected to power. The tides had turned, but General Francisco Franco stationed in the Canary Islands, realised his opportunity for power had come. Franco had thousands of Spanish and Moorish trained soldiers at his disposal in Morocco. A deal was struck with Adolf Hitler. In return for supplies of Spain's natural resources, which Hitler needed for his own future war, Germany would fly Franco's troops into Spain. Not only did Franco agree to the terms, but he later welcomed the aid the German Air Force with the bombing of Guernica, the first time any European civilians had been slaughtered and targeted from the air. Not only did the Luftwaffe obliterate the town with bombs, but low-level flying allowed the machine-gunning of civilians. Guernica had given the German air force an opportunity to practise warfare under real conditions. Men, women, and children were being killed by Germans again, less than 20 years after the end of World War One. Mussolini also enabled Franco's Nationalists by sending 80,000 troops. Still the British and the French governments followed their policy of appeasement. Newsreel film of the bombings and the death toll on civilians was shown to audiences in cinemas all over the world. The reaction by unionists and ordinary people was one of solidarity.

Shocked by the horrors that were taking place,

Liverpool workers organised protest rallies and meetings. Collections were carried out in factories, and a Liverpool chartered ship was laden with food and sailed to Spain. Spanish and Basque orphaned evacuee children were aided by political and church groups. The Spanish Civil War had become a fight for working class people and seen as a stand against the threat of European fascism. A call for physical help came from the Republican government, and 130 able bodied Merseyside men defied their government and set off to take up arms in defence of Spanish democracy. My dad, Denis Peter Mooney, aged 28 of Anfield, was one of those men. Thirty of their number would never see the River Mersey again, and their shallow graves would remain unmarked in the parched earth of Spain. I do not know if my dad and his best friend went to Spain alone, or whether they were both in an organised group. I do know that the many who left were closely monitored by British Secret Agents, as what they were doing was seen as illegal.

Most of the volunteers used a short-term British Visitors Passport to enter France, and the normal route taken was to catch the train/ferry from Victoria to Paris Gare du Nord Station. Once in France's capital the volunteers had an address to go to where they, along with thousands from all over the globe, were enrolled into The International Brigade. It is estimated that their numbers rose to 40,000 in total.

Another long train journey awaited them, this time to the Spanish border town of Perpignan. There they were met by Spanish couriers who explained the journey that lay ahead. They would be led through the passes and rock faces of the Pyrenees Mountains, which were monitored by French border guards and their dogs.

Always guarded in his recollections of Spain, there was one little humorous tale he told of his arrival in Spain. Having crossed the channel, the full length of France, and the Pyrenees mountains he asked his Spanish group leader for food and was unceremoniously thrown an onion! One lesson my dad learned more than any other in Spain was comradeship. He found himself actively involved with men like himself. He also learned that a man should never judge another by the colour of his skin, for amongst his number were many black Americans, and black French. It was a good and healthy lesson to learn, and one he abided by all his life. That is where my knowledge of my dad's time in Spain ends. Why? It is quite simple; apart from a few little tales, my dad never told us anything.

So, this is my own personal vision of how to explain my dad's reluctance to talk. He had been raised on tales of the nobility of warfare. He was to learn otherwise in

Spain, for there is little glory fighting in the insanity of a civil war. It would be unimaginable to comprehend what he saw and possibly participated in. It was a war of family against family, led often by undisciplined untrained civilians, dressed in the barest of uniforms. Retributions took place, and grievances were met with a bullet or torture. Neither side were innocent, and it is estimated that over 200,000 died as a result of mob violence and systematic killings. Women Republicans suffered head shavings, rape, sexual abuse, and murders carried out by Franco's followers, and the Moorish troops he had brought with him from North Africa. The General condoned such behaviour towards his women enemies, declaring in one of his speeches: 'Our brave Legionnaires and Regulares have shown the red cowards what it means to be a man. Kicking their legs about and squealing won't save them.'

Such horrors would have a terrible effect on any decent human being. The danger was that such cruelties would also bring out the worst in retribution. Barbarism was not just dispelled by Fascists; Republicans were also guilty of terrible atrocities. They had been robbed by the landowners and kept down by the church all their lives, and the executions of priests and the burning of churches became regular occurrences.

With arms supplied from Germany and Italy, and

knowing his adversaries were ill equipped, Franco knew he would eventually crush the socialists. No aid came to the Republicans who continued to believe that the British or French would help. In 1939 it was over, and Franco declared himself as supreme leader. He was not finished with his enemies however, and it is estimated that his retribution cost the lives of a further 100,000. The International Brigade had been disbanded the year before in the October. This occurred on the orders of Juan Negrin, the Spanish Prime Minister. He had done so in the forlorn hope that the Nationalists would do the same with their foreign soldiers, which totalled between 40 and 50 thousand Italian and German personnel. A special farewell ceremony was organised in Barcelona to thank and say farewell to the men and women who had left their own countries to fight for the Republic. Dolores Ibarruri Gomez, one of the Republics top politicians who was known as 'the passionate one,' made a speech of thank you that has gone down in history. Here are a few segments of that speech:

'They gave us everything-their youth or their maturity, their science or their experience, their blood and their lives, their hopes and aspirations-and they asked us for nothing. Mothers! When the rancours have died out and pride in a free country is felt equally by all Spaniards, speak to your children. Tell them of these men of The International

Brigades. Recount for them how, coming over seas and mountains, crossing frontiers bristling with bayonets, sought by raving dogs thirsting to tear their flesh, these men reached our country as crusaders for freedom, to fight and die for Spain's liberty threatened by German and Italian fascism. They gave up everything-their loves, their countries, home and fortune, fathers, mothers, wives, brothers, sisters and children-and they said 'We are here. Your cause is ours. It is the cause of all advanced and progressive mankind. Today many are departing. Thousands remain, shrouded in Spanish earth. You are history. You are legend. You are the heroic example of democracy's solidarity. We shall not forget you, and when the olive tree of peace is in flower-return. Return to our side, for here you will find a homeland-all will have the affection and gratitude of the Spanish people who today and tomorrow will shout with enthusiasm-Long live the heroes of the International Brigade.'

I find such a tribute to men like my dad very moving. The man who gave me life had something inside him that felt deeply about injustice, decency, and humanity. So strong were those beliefs that he crossed over Europe and trudged across mountains that were patrolled by men and dogs. He never openly spoke of his actions, just did what he felt was right, and chose to keep his council. To me he was a true hero, a man who risked his life to help his fellow man and sadly failed. It was a portion of his life he wanted to keep to himself, and one that makes me proud to have been his son.

Whilst in Spain he had been hospitalised with a shrapnel wound in his leg, a misfortune that would make him ineligible for service in 1939 at the outbreak of the war caused by a world's unwillingness to curtail the obvious threat of fascism.

If the efforts of the Brigade volunteers were appreciated in Spain, there would be no throwing of flowers or hero's welcome once over the border in France. Considered by the French as an embarrassment, they were placed in border camps. A short while later my dad and his comrades were unceremoniously loaded onto trains bound for Paris. The only source of food given on the long journey was provided by The Salvation Army, who provided them with hot soup at various stations along the way. The same kind of welcome awaited my dad in Liverpool. He and his pal arrived exhausted late one evening in Lime Street Station without a penny between them. After saying their farewells, the two men set off in opposite directions for the long walks that lay ahead. Though they knew their son was coming home, that was the only information my grandparents had been able to acquire. Being awoken at two in the morning by a knock on their front door brought great relief to both. My dad, always one to be so smart and tidy, was a pitiful sight to see. He was gaunt and dishevelled and had an unpleasant smell! After his years in combat, and understanding his son's plight, my grandfather realised that his son had lice and he told his wife to quickly run a hot bath, and to dig out the strongest soap she could find. He also told his son to remove his clothing which he quickly burned in the still flickering embers of the kitchen fire. Later that morning a shaved and thoroughly washed and fed Denis Peter Mooney slept in his first proper bed since he had been hospitalised several months before. It was a sleep that lasted over twelve hours.

He was soon to learn that Liverpool employers were not interested in men who had gone abroad to fight for foreigners, and who the right-wing press called troublemakers. Such papers as *The Daily Mail* even went as far as to describe the volunteers as traitors. There was a reason for such hostility in the newspaper. Its owner, Lord Rothermere, made no secret of his admiration for Hitler stating that the Nazis 'represent the birth of Germany as a nation,' and featured vile editorials with headlines like 'Hurrah for the Blackshirts!' While the Nazis were openly being hostile to the Jews, and opening concentration camps (church burning, banning them from parks, concerts, cinemas, theatres, government jobs, medical and legal practices,) the Daily Mail was printing headlines that complained about the number of Jews 'Pouring into this country.' Sadly, not a lot has changed on the front page of that newspaper since the 1930s, as a recent headline described immigrants as 'The swarm on our streets.'

It took seventy years for those brave men who left their homes to fight in Spain to get the recognition that was so prevalent in 1938. Ninety percent of them were dead before the Spanish government awarded the handful still alive full Citizenship, and a Spanish passport, which incidentally my brothers and myself could apply for and receive. The recognition of such an award would have meant so much to my dad. In my mind, he was disillusioned by the fact that so many of his comrades were killed, not just by fascists, but by the indifference of Britain and France. Disillusioned that so few were concerned or interested in a war that governments knew Hitler and Mussolini were helping finance.

A plaque now hangs on the wall in Liverpool's Town Hall in commemoration of the 400 Merseyside men who fought in Spain. Whilst I am appreciative, it would have meant more to me and my brothers if it had been placed there before so many, like my quiet and reserved father, had died. In the weeks and months that followed his return my dad took whatever work he could acquire, including a stint as the uniformed doorman at Lewis's store. Hardly the kind of job suited to someone who had the benefit of an education in Liverpool's best school. The truth was that he was in no position to do otherwise. And I would imagine he pondered many times wondering if his time in Spain had been worth the human cost. One year after his return from Spain, Germany attacked Poland and Britain declared war on The Third Reich. There are historians who believe that the Second World War could have been delayed, if not avoided, had the Republic of Spain been supplied with arms, as the Germans and Italians had done for Franco's Nationalists. The thinking behind such reasoning was that Hitler would have seen some kind of signal that his two adversaries were not as weak as he perceived them to be. I do not know, but I do know that I had a father who was willing to fight and die for a nation that needed help to retain a democratically elected government. Such men are rare, and it fills me with pride knowing that my dad was such a man.

MY MATERNAL SIDE
JOHN KENYON SNR (1854-not known)

John Kenyon Snr (1810-1883) arrived in Merseyside sometime during the Industrial revolution. He had left Rainford, a small town famous for its manufacture of clay pipes. He met and married Alice Rogers (1812-1890) and the couple settled in Seaforth on the opposite banks of the Mersey to Liverpool.

MARINER FOR WALLASEY FERRIES
JOHN KENYON JNR AND ELLEN EVANS

Sadly, I do not know the birthdate or death date for John Jnr. I assume that he was born around the Seaforth region because his whole life was spent as a ferryman on the river. Ellen Ann Jones married John in Liverpool. She was a Welsh girl from the small North Wales town of Abergele. She would have been very conversant with the Welsh language, as Abergele would have only become more Anglified with the coming of the railway in 1848.Surrounded by hills, a castle, and iron age forts, the small town, and its close proximity to a beautiful beached coastline proved very popular with north west visitors. Beautiful as it was, Ellen was obviously a girl who had wider horizons. Why, or how, Ellen went to Liverpool is lost to history, but she most certainly took her staunch chapel religious beliefs with her.

MARGARET KENYON (1881- 1970)

Better known to her grandchildren as Aunty Maggie, (due to her abhorrence of old age), our grandmother used to turn up her nose and brag as if it made her upper class 'I'm not from Liverpool, I'm from Cheshire.' Indeed, she had been born in Seacombe. The older of two sisters, she grew up in an unhappy household. Her mother was overly religious, and her father was seemingly paranoid about his daughters playing with friends that included boys. When we were kids, she often told us stories regarding her father's delusional and manic behaviour. From the decks of the ferry, he could see her playing on the promenade that led to New Brighton and misinterpreted her innocent play as reckless. He would accuse her of being promiscuous at a time and an age when she was just enjoying her friends. Making her life just as difficult was an overtly religious mother who ensured that both of her daughters attended church three times every Sunday.

Aged just fourteen, my Aunty Maggie could take no more and left for Liverpool. Somehow, known only to history, she had acquired a job in service in Liverpool. She lived to be 79 years old, but in all the years that followed she never crossed the Mersey back to Seacombe. She did tell us that she learned that her father was held responsible for a collision of the ferry and was demoted. The disgrace became too much for him, and I believe that he had a nervous breakdown. He was eventually committed to what was then known as The County Lunatic Asylum in Rainhill near St Helens. Possibly the indignity led to seizures, but from what Aunty Maggie told her grandsons, I think it is safe to say he already had mental problems. I do not know for sure, but I think he remained institutionalised for the rest of his life.

'MAD SAM' – YORKSHIRE POLICE/FIREMAN SAMUEL WALKER (1827-1906)

Sam was born in Linthwaite near Huddersfield, Yorkshire. I am not sure when he left Yorkshire, but he married Miss Elizabeth Redhead in Liverpool in 1856. Sam had joined the Liverpool Police Force some time earlier and was stationed in the Kirkdale area. At that time, the police and Fire Service were united. Later in Sam's life he was stationed at a building which has now been altered into apartments. 'The Old Bill' as it is still known, had facilities for both police and the fire service, with its horse drawn tenders. Samuel Walker was the driver of one of those tenders, and such was the speed that he drove his horses, that he became known locally as 'Mad Sam.' Sam and Elizabeth had one child in 1858 who they named George.

GEORGE WALKER (1858-1944)

I have not been able to find out anything regarding the man who was my great grandfather other than his birth date, marriage, and death. He seems to have lived a long life. Married Sarah Jane Lloyd in 1882.

GEORGE WALKER (1884 -1944)

The first information I have of my grandfather was that he joined the Royal Navy at the age of 18 and remained for four years on board HMS Vivid, later renamed HMS

Dartmouth. He married my grandmother in 1908. In 1914 George was once again in uniform, but this time it was the khaki of the army. He served his country in France between 1914 and 1916. In civilian life, he had been employed as a painter but later built up a large round as a window cleaner. Strangely, he died the same year as his aged father.

VIOLET WALKER (1911-2006)

Aged just three, my mam would have been just getting to know her father when he was sent to France. Away for two years, he would have returned to his home as a stranger. He was fortunate, not just to have survived, but to have kept his mental health.

The Walker family grew, and my mam was joined by two brothers and a sister. I know little of my mams early years other than it was her job to take her siblings three times to church each Sunday and that her dad had enrolled her in The Orange Lodge. She married sometime in her twenties and became a Mrs Myers. The marriage was sadly interrupted when her first husband got sick and became another victim of the dreaded killer of the time tuberculosis. She nursed him in every capacity until the end.

Brother George was first on the scene. He grew up as a bit of a tear away. He was motorbike crazy and seems to have spent his teens messing about with, and racing motor high speed bikes. So much so that he got himself in trouble with the police on more than one occasion. I think he also may have done speed track racing also, as I know my mam mixed with speedway lads. Sadly, younger brother Alfie suffered from tuberculosis most of his life, but he was never left out of anything, and the two were renowned for tearing at high speed around the streets of Kensington.

An appearance in Dale Street Magistrates Court was to be a cathartic experience for young George. The war had only just started, and George had yet to be called up. The magistrate seems to have been a 'wise old owl'. Choosing his words, he reminded George that his country needed young men with zeal and zest, and that he was better serving his country than serving time. He warned George that he was giving him one last chance, and if he saw him again, he would put him away. George joined The Red Berets, and would later be dropped into Arnhem in Holland, famously portrayed in the Richard Attenborough film 'A Bridge Too Far.' After he was demobbed, he gave my mam his parachute. Made of silk, the chute was converted into the curtains that hung in our Garston bedrooms. While still in uniform, George married, left Liverpool, and became a coal miner in Wigan. He never returned, but I do recall one visit to Wigan that my mam and dad had taken me on when I was about six. I do not remember any great welcome and recall his wife as being a bit cold and aloof. They had a little girl, and I recall the pair of us were bundled outside to play in the front garden. We never went back, and I never remember there being any contact. Youngest brother Alf suffered terribly during his short life. Tuberculosis played a tragic part in his young life, but George left him out of nothing, often having to carry him. He died in 1944, and my brother John was given the middle name Alfred as a commemoration.

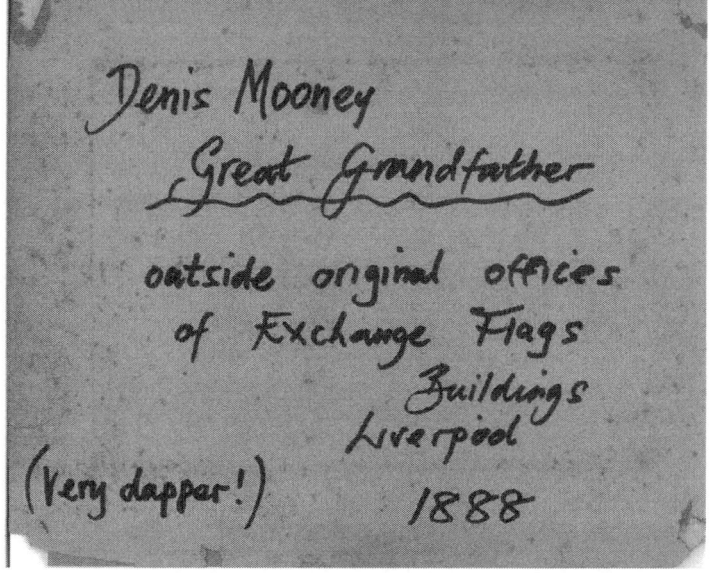

Denis Mooney
Great Grandfather

outside original offices
of Exchange Flags
Buildings
Liverpool

(Very dapper!)
1888

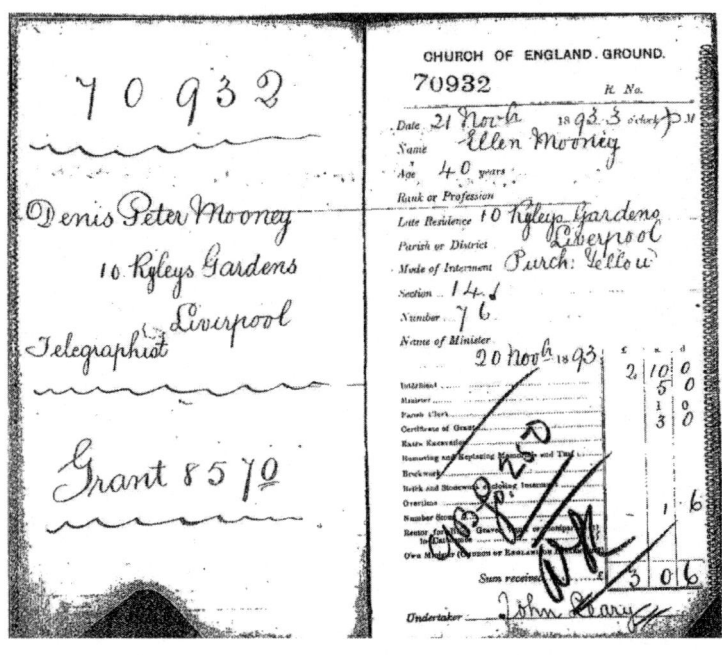

Purchase of plot
of Ellen Mooney (Gt grandmother)
1893

Sgnt Major Denis Mooney (Third from the right with baton) 1915. Tenby, Wales.
Pembrokeshire Yeomanry.

Penally Camp. Tenby, Wales. Pembrokeshire Yeomanry.

Sgnt Major Denis Mooney leading his troops across Libyan Desert. 1917.

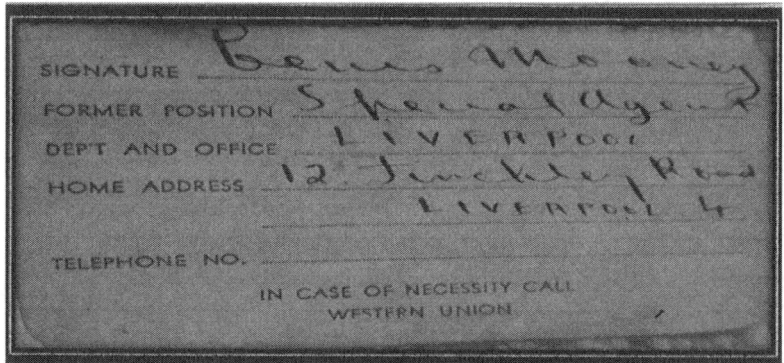

Denis Mooney. Special Agent for Western Union.

Denis Mooney. 1881-1958. Retirement Photos 1936 from Western Union.

LIVERPOLITAN.

July, 1936

MR. DENIS MOONEY,
Hon. Secretary,
West Derby Liberal Assoc.

* * *

LIVERPOOL ECHO

April 5th 1958

City J.P. Is
Found Dead

Soldier And
Sportsman

For over 20 years a Liverpool magistrate, Mr. Denis Mooney was found dead at his home, 12 Finchley Road, Anfield, yesterday. The discovery was made by his son.

Mr. Mooney became a J.P. in 1936, two years before his retirement from the Western Union with whom he spent thirty-five years.

He was born in Dublin, coming to Liverpool at an early age with his parents. In his youth he attempted to join the Klondyke Gold Rush but was unable to raise the necessary money.

Still in search of adventure he volunteered for service in the Boer War and was promoted Troop Sergeant Major on the field for gallantry. In 1916 he was in the Libyan Desert with Allenby and then on to Suez and Palestine where he was mentioned in despatches. His interest in Army life continued and in 1938 he prompted the move to re-form the Irish Battalion of the King's (Liverpool) Regiment. In 1938 he got the agreement of Mr Hore Belisha and the battalion were eventually re-formed in 1947.

Mr Mooney was a president of the Liverpool Irish Old Comrades Association.

A keen sportsman he was closely associated with the Everton Baseball Club of which he was chairman for a number of years.

Mr Mooney was a widower.

71

Leslie Mooney with a woman in a bar or nightclub (Approx. 1939-1940)

Bryan Mooney. Palestine. 1936.

Bryan Mooney. Years Unknown.

Helen Mooney with daughter Helen (Gi
1954.

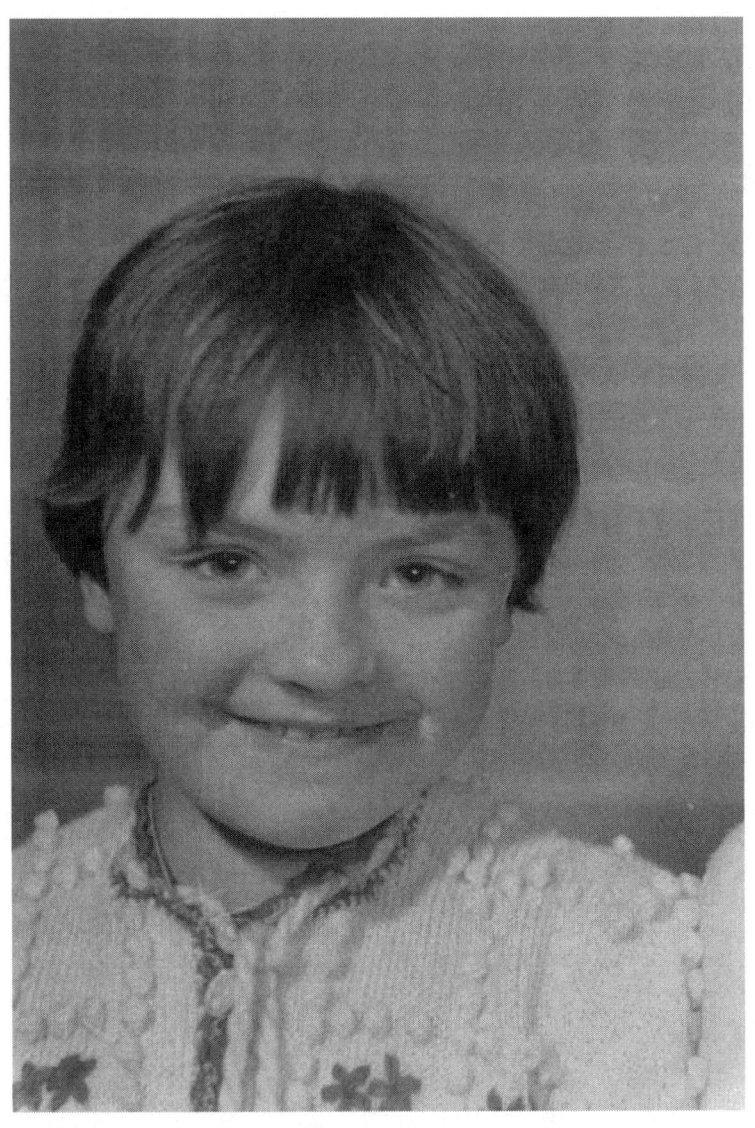

Helen (Girlie) Mooney

Girlie's Grave

Bryan Mooney playing at The Prospect of Whitby, Wapping. Mid-1950's.

John, Denis and Brian Mooney. Taken at their Grandfather's house. 1951.

Top of King Street, Garston. (Year Unknown)

Denis Peter Mooney (Brian's Father) 1960.

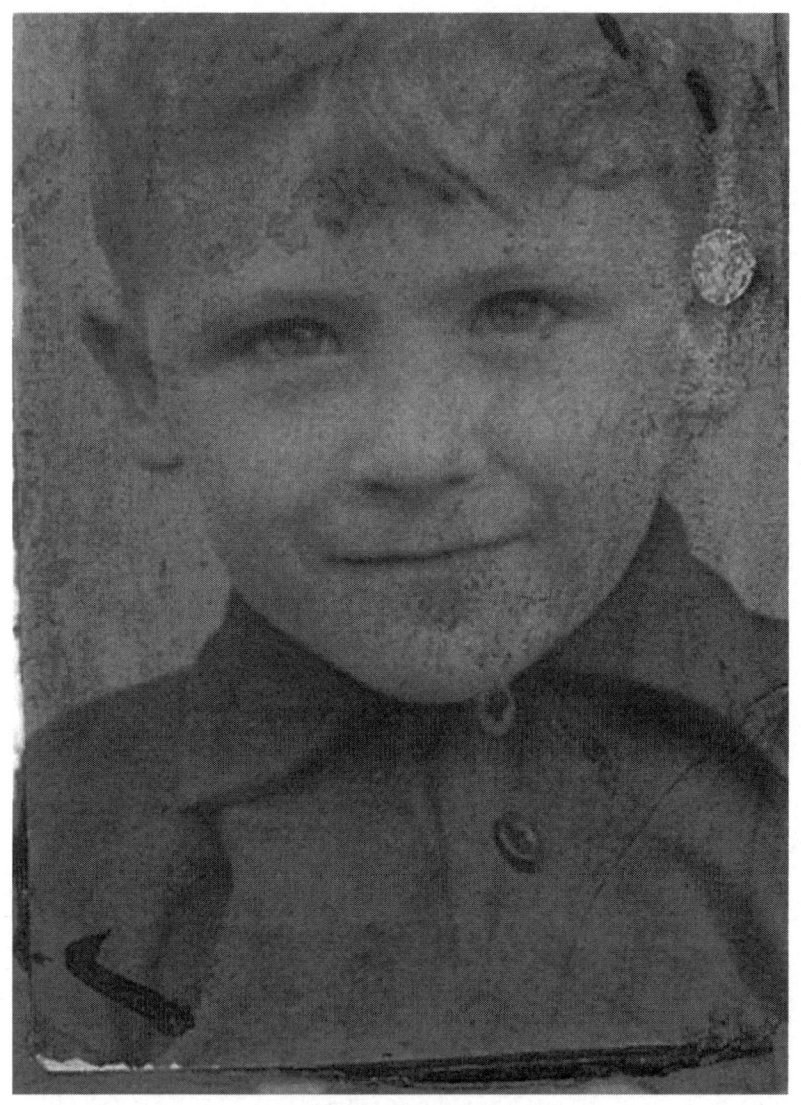

Brian Mooney (Author) 1950.

Violet, Denis, John and Brian (in pram). Garston, Liverpool. 1947.

1940 – FAIRGROUNDS, ROMANCE, AND 166 GERMAN BOMBERS

In 1939 and through to the late summer of 1940, Merseyside remained unscathed from German bombers. People were prepared as much as they could be, and all were fully aware that at any moment Liverpool would be a prime target.

Like his father before him, my dad was a fine-looking man, well mannered, and always careful in his appearance and with his words. His accent was best described as refined Liverpool, and it was obvious to all he met that he had received a good education. From time to time his age, and the fact that he was not in uniform caused unpleasant scenes. Sometimes he would be aware of older men deliberately brushing past him or feel the stares of people he did not know. He knew that they thought him to be a conscientious objector. He must have wanted to scream at them of where he had been, and what he had put himself through. Obviously, he could do nothing of the sort but live with the truth and say nothing.

In the summer of 1940, he had found himself in some sort of supervisory position in offices downtown. Part of his duties was to ensure the cleaners did a thorough job. He had obviously set his sights on one of his cleaning girls, for he had waited for Violet Myers to finish her work, and asked if he could see her home.

Violet was more than happy to accept Denis's offer, especially with the threat of an air raid hanging over civilian lives. They must have hit it off because a date for the following Wednesday was set for a night out across the river in New Brighton.

The summer was drawing to a close, but the ferry crossings to the seaside resort were still unabated and Denis and Violet were enjoying each other's company. They did what most couples would have done and spent time in the fairgrounds and pubs along the promenade. The war seemed so far away in the New Brighton of 1940, which boasted the largest outdoor swimming pool in the country, as well as the beach and numerous dance halls.

Their enjoyment, and that of their fellow day-trippers, was cut short that night by the warning sound of air raid sirens. Fortunately, New Brighton had several tunnels that dated back to the town's period of smuggling and piracy. Presumably, that is where the panicking people ran, as a loud drone came from the skies. It is difficult in today's world to contemplate the sheer horror that must have overcome ordinary people during such traumatic events. One hundred and sixty-six German bombers were paying their first major bombing visit to Merseyside. Luckily, the pleasure resort of New Brighton was of no interest to them, for their target on that pleasant late summer night were the docks of Birkenhead.

I do not know how long a raid of so many planes would take to fly over the river and drop their bombs, but those cowering in the air raid shelters were getting their first taste of what lay in store for well over another year. Later that night, after the all clear had been sounded, people emerged from the shelters to see the full extent of what bombs can do. The sky was black with smoke and red with fire. People flocked to the promenade and pier to get a better look at what the Germans had done in one brief raid. People began wandering around aimlessly, obviously realising that there was no possibility of the ferries still running, Denis and Vi found a promenade bench. Watching the flames was the way my parents spent their first night together. My mam would joke later that my dad was a perfect gentleman, as indeed he always was.

The raid that night was followed by fifteen more raids in September and nine in October. On November the 28th and 29th, 350 tons of high explosive bombs, 3,000 incendiaries, and 30 land mines were dropped on Liverpool, bringing about the deaths of 300 people. Such raids were increased in 1941, making Liverpool the second highest bombed city in England.

Had they not realised it before, my parents

concluded that lives had to be lived in the moment. The war was going badly, and Britain stood alone. The German army had conquered France, Belgium, Holland, and Poland. My dad was well aware that if the Germans conquered Britain, as they had every indication of doing, he would be a marked person. His Spanish escapade would definitely have led to his arrest, with only one outcome. He knew what the Nazis did to their political opposites, and it would not have taken them long to have found him out. Denis and Violet must obviously have discussed such matters, and decided there was no time to be wasted. Three weeks later they tied the knot.

Both were from the north of the city, so their first married abode was in a flat in Everton. I know nothing about this period other than my eldest brother Denis was born in the summer of 1942, a year after the bombing of Pearl harbour by Japan. My dad initially was doing his bit in a variety of Civil Defence jobs.

At some stage he managed to acquire a position working for the Admiralty. This was more in keeping with his education. It would have been some form of clerical work, and he was stationed in The Naval Stores in Window Lane, Garston.

GARSTON, AND THE LAST STREET BEFORE THE DOCKS

By 1943 the German bombers had switched their attention eastward. They had left behind Britain's second most bombed city. The British and U.S. air forces had turned the tables and were now pounding German cities. The war was beginning to turn. With the entry of America into the war, and with Russia draining the manpower of the German war machine, it was no longer a question of if Germany could be defeated, but just how long it would take.

Though Garston was an area quite alien to my dad, he was told of a house for rent in a nearby street. Living in a cramped flat with a baby boy was hardly ideal, so the chance of a house, any house, seemed a good solution. Though many miles from their own part of the city, both my parents felt it to be worth the disruption.

Garston, like much of the city had taken the full brunt of German bombs, especially around the dock area. Shand Street was a row of less than 40 terraced houses that had been built to accommodate the incoming newly required workers in the 1870's. Each house consisted of two bedrooms, a front parlour, and a small kitchen. At the rear was an outside toilet, and a small yard that opened out to a back entry. Like most

Garston streets it had been hit by a bomb, leaving a cratered area where two houses once stood. Number 34 lay at the bottom of the cul-de-sac, only separated from the dock by a corrugated iron boundary and several large molasses tanks. The street had been built quickly and cheaply with everything being at its most basic. The area was known as 'under the bridge' by Garstonians, as it was separated from Garston village by a railway bridge and consisted of two main thoroughfares both ending at the Mersey.

King Street was the closest of them to the docks, and Shand Street was at its base. Window Lane was the busier of the two thoroughfares and had more in the way of shops. Such was the population 'under the bridge' that it sustained three fish and chip shops, a Chinese laundry, a Co-op, a bakery, a chemist, a wool shop, a lady's hairdressers, a pet shop, two newsagents, a butcher's shop, two barbers, and several well utilised pubs. Though King Street shops were of the more basic type, they catered for the everyday needs of the residents. Window Lane was also busy enough to have had a bus service, the number 66 which ran to Woolton.

My dad had been raised in a middle-class house in Anfield. It is still standing today, a testament to its quality. A grammar schoolboy, he had been raised comfortably as the first born of a stern but loving father, and a very doting mother. He was raised to have active mind, and to use every opportunity to further his knowledge of both the city, and world events.

Moving into a tiny dockside house that had no bathroom, and an outside toilet would not have been to my dad's taste. He also had little in common with neighbours who were dockers, merchant seamen, or native Garstonians. Beggars cannot be choosers however, and it was what it was. He chose therefore to keep himself to himself and never frequented the public houses, though I was told that before marriage he could take his ale with the best of them.

Garston was not so difficult for my mam whose life had never been anything but difficult, so she concentrated on being a wife, a mother, and a good neighbour. The family increased with the arrival of John in the summer of 1944.My dad had some very old-fashioned ideas, with his attitude to a woman's place. When they married, he would say 'No wife of mine will ever work!' That was a very sweeping, but also a very ill-thought-out statement to make to my strong-willed mother. It therefore came as quite a shock to him one night when he returned home to find his wife with dark yellow powder in her hair. He was brought off his high horse on being told that the family needed money, and that she had become what they called a 'Canary Girl' in a munitions factory. Incidentally, that work ethic, and her belief in 'no one gets anything for nothing,' was the mainstay of her life, not giving up work till she was 84.

1945 saw the folks of Shand Street celebrating Victory in Europe day. The war in Europe was over, and so too was the need for Canary Girls, and work done by the Liverpool Admiralty staff. There was work to be found, and both had no problems finding other jobs.

As was envisaged, a Socialist government was voted in with a massive majority. Winston Churchill had been the man of his time, but people wanted radical change. He had led the nation through the worst of times, and such people were necessary to hold the country together. However, in reality, he represented a class system that the British people wanted rid of. The men and women who had given their everything for nearly six years wanted a newer and less class driven Britain. The incoming Labour Party was faced with a nation that was virtually bankrupt. Drastic measures were needed, and drastic measures were taken. The railways, steel, coal, and civil aviation were all nationalised. A 'Welfare State' was created with the ideal of British people becoming part of an equal society. Social reform was the new priority, and would affect every man, woman, and child. Most radical was the creation of a The National Health Service giving every citizen the right of care at the point of need. $3.75 billion dollars repayable back over 50 years was loaned by the U.S.

government, and not paid in full until 2006, by another Labour government.

The post war years were extremely difficult for everyone, but whatever money the government held was being fairly used and distributed. Such challenging times for the Mooney family were probably not helped by my arrival in the autumn of 1946.

FROM A QUIET VILLAGE TO A HIVE OF INDUSTRY

The Garston we had been born into, like the rest of Liverpool, had grown up in a hurry, primarily after the mid-19th century. Its expansion and development occurred quickly after the creation of several new docks, the 'Old Dock' in 1846, and the 'North Dock' twenty years later. The rapid development of railroad lines gave the docks easy access to other parts of the northwest, thereby initially allowing them to be utilised for the transportation of coal and other essential cargoes to Ireland.

Prior to that period, Garston had little industry other than a salt works with a small dock, and a few brick works. The land was still utilised by tenant farmers, and it was classified as a village on the outer boundaries of southern Liverpool. With the opening of the new docks came the workers. There was no shortage of labour, especially after the terrible potato famine had left thousands of Irish immigrants in the seaport. Rapidly needed houses were built. It was the Irish who gained the majority of jobs in the new Garston Docks, many coming from the Wicklow area of Ireland, and consisted of many who were related. This caused problems and unrest, with the infamous tally men said to be favouring their own.

The success of the docks saw small and large industries moving into what rapidly became a critical area of industry for the seaport. Other labour arrived from Wales and the surrounding counties of Liverpool. Those newcomers tended to work in the factories that were opening. One of those new industries was The Garston Bobbin Works, a huge factory which gave work for hundreds of both men and women. In the years that followed, The Garston Bottle Works, The Bryant and May Match works, The Garston Gasworks, and The Garston Tanning Company emerged, all providing good solid employment for future generations of Garstonians.

On the other side of the Church Road bridge, was the village, and the quality of the housing was comparatively better, with some houses having three bedrooms, and some even having indoor bathrooms. The main thoroughfare into the Garston village area was St Mary's Road, coming as it did from the heart of the city. Over time it was to become Garston's High Street with banks, hotels, pubs, and retail outlets of every description. More amenities arrived as Garston grew and the years past. Two cinemas (one of which had been built as a variety theatre) and a public swimming pool and bathhouses were built, plus a large hospital. There were pubs galore, of the basic watering hole variety, and Garston's workers kept such establishments well utilised.

OLD TIME RELIGION

Religion was far more important back then especially with the arrival of so many Irish Catholics. Garston had been a predominantly Protestant village with St Michael's Anglican Church as its Centrepoint. With everyone basically being in the same boat, a quiet acceptance of people's differing religious beliefs gradually set in. People brought their own denominations with them and before long they had erected their own churches and chapels.

From my memory people tolerated their neighbours in the open but spoke derogatory words of prejudice about them at home. Human nature being what it is, mixed marriages invariably took place, which sadly sometimes led to family break ups and confrontation. As with other parts of the city, The Orange Lodge with its pipe bands and drums boomed out on the important days in its calendar. To me, the celebration of battles fought hundreds of years before seemed a pointless exercise, but their Garston piped band played and marched with real belief.

Thankfully, organised religion was not a subject of any relevance to the Mooney family. We had no prejudices that I can remember, and I can never recall my mam talking badly of others. She did however try her best to bring some form of belief in her boys by sending us to Sunday School. We only went the once, and she never forced the issue. We did however attend St Michael's each Christmas morning. It became a ritual, and we boys just fell in line without objection, besides, we liked singing carols. My dad never attended, and though he was very much an atheist, he never objected, or was ever critical of my mam's efforts.

Transportation into the main city area improved over time with the introduction of excellent train, tram, and later bus services. Garston was a place of work and factories and officially became part of Liverpool at the beginning of the 20th century. So, that was the Garston of my birth. An industrial dockland of gaslit and cobbled streets, tiny, terraced houses, and mixed religions. An area of Liverpool divided by a railway bridge into two vastly different regions. An area full of post war kids, who could enjoy the freedom of streets with few cars, and an undeveloped riverside world that was paradise for active 'scallywags.'

SHAND STREET LIFE, BANANAS, AND FAMILY SUNDAYS

To be born 'under the bridge' that divided the docks, from what is still called the village, identified you as being a 'Mudman.' I think it is a relatively new term as I don't remember it from my childhood. It is a very, very apt description. Anyway, whether new or old, for better or worse, that is what I am. I wear the title as a badge of honour. To me the name was earned by being a kid who got filthy most days playing alongside a river that was dead. A river bordered by beaches of muddy sludge created by 100 years of industrial pollution. Yet we thought nothing of it. I will deal in more depth about going 'down the shore' later, for that shoreline was an essential part of my childhood.

Strange, but I can never remember being envious of others or wishing for more. We had the most basic of everything, but our lives were rich in so many ways. Number 34 Shand Street was no different from the other houses in the nearby dockland streets. They were minimal, and well past their usage. Though they were old and without merit, the women always kept them as welcoming and clean as they could. Every doorstep was regularly scrubbed, and the front parlours were pristine with whatever presentable furniture could be afforded.

Our own parlour had a table, four chairs, a dresser for photos, and a wind-up gramophone that I never remember working. The parlour was virtually out of bounds to us brothers and was always clean in case someone cared to call. Strangely very few ever did, apart from the two life insurance men who came for their weekly collection of one shilling. Each always had the time for a chat with my mam and were the recipients of a hot cup of tea.

The upstairs bedrooms had wooden floorboards, and were very, very cold in the winter. Initially we were three brothers in one bed, until eldest brother Denis grew too big and was given a bed of his own. Any heat was provided by blankets and old army overcoats. One brick type hot water bottle was always fought over by cold feet. There was no light upstairs, so going to bed in winter was done with the aid of a candle. I can still picture the three of us using the candle and our hands to create animal figures in the shadows. Definitely a world before health and safety. There was a large world map on the bedside wall and Denis, who always had a mind for facts, would test his two younger brothers on capital cities.

As stated, there was no light upstairs, and downstairs any lighting came from gas mantles, one for the kitchen, and one for the front parlour. The tiny kitchen was our living area, our eating place, our washing place, and more importantly, the place where my dad taught us how to play cards. It is also the place where my mam received a regular visit from a group of lads selling big stalks of bananas. I do not know how often the Fyffes banana ships docked in Garston, but strangely at a cost of 2 shillings and sixpence per long stalk, some always found their way to the back door of number 34. My dad, who was honest as the days were long, always objected to her buying stolen goods. My mam would tell him in no uncertain terms that she was feeding her kids. Well, as an old man today, I can say that I had bananas coming out my ears back then and barely touch them now. It was fried bananas for breakfast, banana butties at dinnertime, and bananas and custard for tea!

The kitchen area was where my mam washed us brothers in the large enamel sink each morning. As the smallest child, I was normally lifted and placed at the side of the sink for my daily bish bash bosh of carbolic soap, making me smell like 1 had just come out of Garston hospital. Placed in the centre of the kitchen, directly in front of the coal fire, was my dad's armchair. He was a very patient father because most nights he would allow me to stand behind him and comb his hair into amazing but crazy hairstyles while he read his Liverpool Echo. He was always particularly good at sketching, something he handed down to me. He did not draw for himself, but for his sons. Best of all were his drawings of liners, which I am sure reminded him of his younger days. He was also very adept at drawing the faces of 1930s movie glamour girls.

It was while sitting in his chair on a Monday night in late January 1953 that my dad read to us of the terrible fire that had destroyed The Empress of Canada in Gladstone Dock. I can still picture him sitting in front of the fire and showing his boys the front-page photos of the 20,000-ton liner. The fire had been at its worst on Sunday night when the flames were so fierce that firemen had to withdraw from the dock. It would be the following Sunday that we went as a family and viewed the wreckage of the passenger ship from the Overhead Railway.

Sunday was always a special day, for we were together as a family, and weather permitting, we ventured to lots of places of interest both on the outskirts, and within the city. Places I recall were Helsby in Cheshire with its Helter Skelter, or to the museums and the lovely parks so predominant in Liverpool. They were days that were incredibly special to us boys, and my dad seemed always knowledgeable about so many things.

A 'BANKS ROAD SAUSAGE'

My earliest memory was being dragged kicking and screaming into the nursery huts that were stationed next to Banks Road School. In 1950, the Liverpool Corporation must have had a system of free nursery care for working mothers! In the years that followed I graduated from the huts to the infant building, after which I crossed the playground to the main school for juniors. Strangely, my memories of school are few, however I do know that by going to Banks Road Junior School I had become a 'Banks Road Sausage.'

One memory that does remain vivid was wearing a paper mâché dragon's head. It was Empire Day 1953, and I was the front end of the beast that was killed by England's patron saint, St. George. The mask was particularly good, and very realistic. As they do with pretend horses in pantomimes, I was at the front of a long line of boys, covered over to look like a dragon's body and legs. It must have been some kind of play, but as I was five years old, the memory has faded. Strange to think that the sun had not set on Britain's Empire, and that the Union Jack was still so prevalent. Maybe it's just nostalgia, or perhaps people were less cynical, but it was a time of patriotism and pride of being British.

I also have vivid memories of the headmistress, Mrs

Stevens, coming out into the school yard and clanging her hand-held brass bell. The school yard seemed quite large, and at its base there was a brick-built air raid shelter. I remember between the infants and juniors was a canteen. Each of us brothers were given money for school dinners that were always wholesome, tasty, and good. After the meat and two veg, there was a tasty, sweet dish that was also always palatable. This was in the early 1950s, and I must ask the question, where did it all go wrong? I remember the kids being given orange juice full of vitamins, all free, and all supplied by the state. The little bottles of milk each morning was an unquestioned part of every child's life at school. I have no recollection of any kids turning their noses up, just of every bottle being drunk.

MA TOBIN, EVERTON, AND THE THREE BRASS BALLS

Some King Street shops, though not all, had a policy of 'tick.' In essence, they knew and trusted their customers with credit. Ma Tobin, as we affectionately knew her, ran a tiny shop on the corner of Sinclair Street. I was regularly sent because she stocked several important items for the Mooney family; kindling wood, candles, gas mantles, and loose Woodbine ciggies for my dad. There was no shame in asking for such items to be put in her little credit book, and the tiny lady never queered such sales. She always kept her little book at the ready confident that she would be paid promptly on pay day. I can still picture her licking her leaded pencil, and always with a smile. She was Irish, as so many were, and presumably had been in Garston for decades. She was a widow and must have led a sad life. She had one child named John. Not knowing the correct 21st century terminology I shall describe John as very mentally challenged. John was harmless; middle aged, and an absolute Everton fanatic! From the minute he got up, to the minute he went to bed it was Everton, Everton, Everton. Even when he was out, he would be thinking aloud, and his one-sided conversation was always about 'the Blues.' It must have been hard on his mother, though she never showed it, and had the patience of a saint. Other shops hung signs in the doorway or above the till. 'Please do not ask for credit, as refusal often offends.'

Frank Kett was a quietly spoken Jewish man who I believed lived and travelled each day from the Wirral. He was Garston's pawnbroker, and, as such, was an especially important man to 'under the bridge' mothers. My mam was a regular weekly customer to Mr Kett. Some women would hide their faces before going under Mr Kett's three ball brass sign, but my mam had no such hang-ups. The usual days for calling on Mr Kett were Tuesdays or Wednesdays, as by that time my mams purse was virtually empty. I cannot recall what she pawned, but it was probably the same item each week. Mr Kett was always courteous and never once did he show signs of disapproval. He knew he provided a need and never looked down his nose at anyone that I knew of. Some women would frequent his shop and spin him a tale about their husband being sick, and Frank, knowing full well she was after money to feed his drinking or gambling habit, would play along and sympathise. My mam needed those few extra coppers to spend on her three boys, we were never without, and Mr Kett and Ma Tobin always got their money.

THE HEATHENS, THE SCALLIES, AND THE GOSPEL MISSION

Religion 'under the bridge' was always more important to the parents than it ever was to the kids. Once out in the street we were all as one. However we went to separate schools, which oddly enough faced each other in Banks Road. My mucker from next door was John. He was about nine months older than me, and his mother was an Irish born staunch Roman Catholic. Fortunately, she never stopped the friendship of John and me developing. In fact, I spent much of my time next door and can remember many occasions where my dad would have to drag me kicking and screaming and put me on his shoulder to get me to bed. John, being that bit older, was my childhood hero. It was him that showed me the ropes at doing daft things like climbing walls that were built to keep us out, and jumping on the backs of moving lorries as they turned into Window Lane from The Garston Bottle works. The dare was to hang on as long as you could as the lorries speeded up. Climbing down ropes into the docks was another regular pastime. We certainly kept the railway police busy, but luck was always on our side, and once up the rope, it was quickly retrieved leaving the breathless coppers 20 feet below. Getting into scrapes doing stupid things, endangering our lives, was all part of our Garston growing up scenario. John was always the instigator, but he was older than me, and I just followed on happily reaping havoc. We did many other crazy things, but they are best not mentioned. We were scallywags without doubt, but I savour the memory. John has been gone now for several years, but he was an integral part of my childhood, and I am not one to forget.

It is strange but the nearest I ever came near to religion was not in a church, but in a room above Robinsons Greengrocers in Hughes Street. One day a sign had gone up telling the world that an upstairs large room had been opened up as The Garston Gospel Mission. What made it interesting to us kids was that the preacher, a well-known character named Mr Little, was holding a Sunday night child only service and was serving tea and cakes! Well, on the following Sunday night there were dozens of kids (Catholics and Protestants) all queuing up waiting for the doors to open. Mr Little's assistant duly opened the door at six o'clock sharp. After an initial rush to get in, he calmed the kids down and let us in one by one. As the lads entered, they were made to leave their weapons downstairs at the door. By the time we had all got in there was a large heap of bows and arrows, cap guns, and catapults.

True to their word, there was a large table of butties and cakes. There was also a huge kettle simmering away, and lots of cups and plates. It is too many years to remember the sermons, but I certainly remember the songs. They were so different from the hymns we were taught at school; they were happy, they were tuneful, and they were easy to sing. We all threw ourselves into it, as we were thinking about what was on that big table. Well, we must have impressed him as we all got our tea and cakes and could not wait for next week. A problem arose when the priests got to hear of what their flock had done, and the parents were informed. There were some thick ears and a few Hail Mary's dished out in the week that followed and Sunday nights at the mission slowly began to die. It was a shame, as I quite enjoyed the music, and of course the tea and cakes. Mr Little, and his upstairs mission was soon a memory of the past. He was still to be seen however, pacing up and down the Pier Head or at whatever sporting event was on, with his board around his neck proclaiming the coming Armageddon.

THIN WALLS AND AMERICAN POPULAR MUSIC

To me and millions of other post war kids, America was where all the good things came from. Hollywood movies captured our imagination. In glorious technicolour and Cinemascope, we saw the wonders of its cities with their big cars, wide highways, and skyscrapers. We gasped at its mountains, deserts, and frontiers in countless westerns. Everything seemed bigger than life. It also had its popular music that was always far superior to anything coming out of English recording studios. While the B.B.C. were playing records of singers like David Whitfield, Ronnie Hilton, Donald Peers, and Dickie Valentine, the Yanks had invaded the British record scene with Frankie Laine, Guy Mitchell, Frank Sinatra, Doris Day, Vic Damone, Teresa Brewer, and Nat King Cole.

Having no electricity, we were reliant on an accumulator radio with a huge battery that required charging every week. This we did at a local cycle shop near the bridge. We would take it early in the morning and collect it late afternoon. The snag was that most of what you heard on the BBC Light Programme was corny English pop. It was not all bad, but it certainly lacked the quality and feel of American music. My introduction to American music came from John's older brother Michael next door. Unlike ourselves, next door had paid for the luxury of electricity to be installed. John's brother took full advantage, by buying a proper electric record player. His knowledge and love of American popular music was amazing, and the wall between our two houses were thin. At bedtime we three brothers would take an empty tumbler glass upstairs and hold it against the wall. With an ear on the glass and taking it in turn, we were taken into another musical world. We heard Country Music for the first time, and we retained a love of that music for the rest of our lives. There was a definite love of Hank Williams coming through the bedroom wall, a musical genius who died aged just 29 on New Years Eve 1952. Young Hank became a mythical character because his songs were lyrically and melodically the work of a genius. Although he was described at the time as a hillbilly singer, his songs crossed over into other forms of popular music and have been recorded over the years by artists as diverse as Ray Charles, Tony Bennett, Mark Knopfler, Elvis, Louis Armstrong, Jerry Lee Lewis, Frankie Lane, Ry Cooder, Tom Petty, and Roy Orbison.

Those records seeped into the soul of the little boy I was. They stayed with me and opened my ear not just to American music, but to the sound of the guitar. Some twenty years later I would find myself, guitar in hand, singing those songs as a semi-pro in front of a band. Those Hank records had opened my musical mind to those who followed like, Buddy Holly, Chuck Berry, Bill Haley, Little Richard, Jerry Lee Lewis, Eddie Cochran, and Johnny Cash. They all represented America, the country that 1950s British kids were in awe of. There are not words enough to thank those thin walls, and that electric record player.

The average attire for 1950s boys, me included, was a school cap, a pair of short grey flannel trousers held up by a snake belt, grey woollen socks up to the knees, and a pair of black plimsolls. Try then to imagine the jealousy we felt when some lads suddenly appeared in the street wearing American baseball boots (similar to sneakers), blue jeans (almost unavailable in England at that time), and snazzy zip up jackets with New York Yankees written of the back! Well, that is what happened every time a Cunard Yankee father returned home from the States. Many Garston fathers had the wanderlust as young men and had joined the merchant navy. Should they have been lucky enough to be on the Atlantic ships, they always returned home with clothes for the kids.

KIDS WHO WERE FREE TO BE KIDS

To Garston kids, the term going 'down the shore' meant adventure and freedom along the banks of the Mersey between Garston and Speke. Riverside industry ended after Garston docks, and what followed were green fields, small woodlands, farms, ponds, and most importantly, no adults. Going 'down the shore' meant the joy of not being supervised, to a place where there were no adult rules, where boys could be boys and get into dangerous scrapes. A place where lads dared each other into doing crazy things that should never have been contemplated. Grazes, cuts, and sometimes even broken bones were the order of the day. With a spring in our step and a wind in our backs we could reach the shore in ten to fifteen minutes from Shand Street. Our group would increase with several lads from nearby streets tagging along, so we would often be ten or twelve in number.

The first thing we came across on the muddy banks of the Mersey shoreline was The Eleanor. She had been a small cargo ship that was moored in the mud, awaiting her demise from the local scrap merchant. Strangely I do not ever remember seeing any scrap workers, so we had the ship to ourselves for the whole summer of 1954. Conveniently there was a hole in the side which made entry into The Eleanor possible. Though the engine had been ripped out, much of the basic structure was still there. It did not take long before ropes were added enabling kids to reach all parts of the hulk. The whole inside was jagged metal, so bloody legs and hands were a regular occurrence. It is difficult to imagine in today's world that kids were once able to play crazily and unsupervised in such an old dangerous vessel. She was just moored in the mud, and not cordoned off in any way. I have no regrets about having been oblivious to any dangers, they were just part and parcel of the daily life of us Mudmen, and most of us lived to tell the tale!

The Eleanor was moored off what we called the first field during the whole of the summer of 1954. Getting to the second field was easy when the weather was dry, but a nightmare after rain, or if the Mersey had been subjected to intense winds. A narrow pathway with a seawall ran alongside the wired high fence of Speke Airport. Quite often, due to harsh weather or high waves, the path was a 200-yard walk of trying to avoid sludge. That could mean having to balance along the high seawall, yet another additional danger. Thoughts of cleanliness and polished shoes went out the window, but we were Mudmen, and it was what it was! Of course, if the tide was out, we walked beneath the seawall amongst the rocks, pebbles, and the flotsam and jetsam of the Mersey. Once at the second field everything got easier. The airport fence continued, as it ran the full length of what was then called Speke Airport, and John Lennon was still in short grey flannel pants. We walked along a well-trodden track with long green ferns on either side. It was seventy years ago, but I can still hear the song of the skylarks that were so prevalent on the airfield side of the wire fence. The airport was still utilised by the Royal Air Force and being boys, we took an interest in the latest jets taking off and landing. Once past the airport were the grounds of Speke Hall, with its beautiful house dating from Tudor times. The grounds contained ornate gardens, and I think were still privately owned. Obviously, scallywags like us were unwelcome, and naturally its riverside woodland was fenced off. That woodland however was full of bird's nests, and bird's eggs! It took until 1981 for a government to ban the taking of eggs from nests. In the 1950s tens of thousands of boys collected them as a hobby. It all seems cruel today, but we knew no better, and it gave us such enjoyment. We were oblivious to what we were doing. The way of preserving the egg was to prick the top and the base with a sharp needle, hold the egg to the mouth and gently blow, thus removing the yolk. It was a skilful procedure, leaving you with egg on your face if you blew too hard. On his 12th birthday my brother Denis received The Observers Book of Bird's Eggs. Enclosed were paintings of every British bird's egg, with a synopsis on the bird, its habitat, and where in Britain it nested. Such information was invaluable to the lads from 'under the bridge ' who would call at 34 Shand Street with their egg safely wrapped in cotton wool for Denis, and his book, to give an expert appraisal.

Denis had a fine collection of his own and was not averse to climbing 30 or 40 feet to build up his hoard. All were placed neatly and safely into a shoe box lined with cotton wool. That box was still around 50 years later. Once past Speke Hall was what we called the first gully. This was part of a farm and was where we got our springtime frog spawn. For any young 1950s lad the collection of spawn was an essential part of growing up. To see the egg change one stage at a time from egg to a small blob developing legs and a body was a fascinating thing for young inquisitive boys. That was what the shoreline did, it was educational and made lads inquisitive about nature. The shore had rabbits, hedgehogs, and birds of all types. It also had woods and ponds. Those ponds contained fish, the most common, and easiest to put in a jam-jar was the stickleback, a red throated tiddler. After the first gully were fields of farm produce right up to Hale lighthouse. Those fields looked particularly spectacular in summer when they were laden with wheat.

In 1953 the Liverpool Echo showed photos of a whale that had been washed up on the beach near the lighthouse. Years later I was to read that John Lennon and a mate had gone by bike to see the whale, and that Lennon had done a drawing of it and given it to his friend. It turned up sixty years later when his mother was having a clear out. Young John would seem to have been artistic even as a kid. It was not only Lennon that frequented the southern Mersey shore, as both Harrison and McCartney had lived in Speke and spent much of their time as kids playing on the beach at Oglet. Getting back to that poor whale, he did exceptionally well to get so far up the river that was so polluted at that time.

THE BLOOD-SOAKED LION TAMER

It was the Easter Bank Holiday weekend in 1954, and the sun was shining. It was decided that we would go as a family to New Brighton. Liverpool's very own seaside resort was a vastly different place in the 1950s. Few people were lucky enough to go for holiday breaks outside of the city, so a day in New Brighton, or further afield to Southport was a special occasion. Everybody would go across the Mersey by ferry, which was an adventure in itself. In fact, during that decade, it is estimated that 30 million people crossed the river by ferry. Thousands of people packed the floating landing stage at the Pier Head, having bussed in from all over Liverpool. Ferries were going back and forth, but from memory there were no long queues. I had been insistent that John from next door should join us, and surprisingly his mother agreed. It would be a day that we would witness a real scene of horror that none of us would ever forget.

As stated, New Brighton was a bustling place back in those post war years. From the moment one stepped off the Royal Daffodil ferry, the sound of the Wurlitzer boomed out, and the whole pier area was a magical place of fairground activities. I knew that John had never been, so it felt good seeing his happy face. It is too long ago for me to remember the details of the places we visited, or the rides we went on, but what happened in the afternoon is embedded in my mind, here is an abridged account from a local newspaper:

'The opening performance of Wilkie's summer circus at New Brighton last Saturday was marred by a mishap to Ray Walker, a 30-year-old lion tamer, who was attacked and clawed by a two-year-old forest bred lion during her act, which formed the climax of the show. The incident was witnessed by a crowded audience including the Mayor and Mayoress of Wallasey.

Miss Walker, in private life Mrs Michael Lane and the mother of two children, was near the gate of the cage and trying to get the lion on a pedestal when the animal sprang. She was knocked to the ground and badly clawed before attendants outside the cage drove the lion off and allowed Miss Walker to scramble out of the gate with face and clothes covered in blood. She was operated on later at Wallasey Hospital for severe lacerations and a broken jaw. The act has been taken out of the show.'

My recollections are slightly different from that journalistic account. Firstly, is the fact that they were not lions but in fact lionesses. Right from the start of her act Miss Walker seemed to be too aggressive towards the wild beasts. She had a chair which she was using on the animals in an overly aggressive manner, poking and prodding. The lioness in my eyes was defending itself.

It was a long time ago, but my recollection was that she caught the lioness in the mouth with one of the chair legs and it retaliated, as any caged animal reared in the wild would do. Thankfully, circuses that mistreat such creatures are outdated and relegated to history.

They were different times however, humankind has grown up, and the welfare of animals has become far more humane. Miss Walker had the whole side of her face ripped open, and the blood changed the colour of her outfit to a bright red. The one thing that surprises me is that the media coverage was so minimal and matter of fact. The poor beast was probably killed, and Miss Walker would have been disfigured for life. For the event to have been so casually reported, I must presume was that it was considered bad publicity for New Brighton and the powerful Wilkie family who had been responsible for much of the resort's success.

THE STOLEN CAT AND GARSTON'S SILVER SCREENS

Going to the 'flicks' was an essential part of our childhood. There was no such thing as picking out what films you went to see, good or bad, you simply went. Fortunately, the early 1950s was a great period from Hollywood and British studios like Elstree. Comedies and classic war films came out from the company of Britain's J. Arthur Rank. Westerns, musicals, and crime movies came from the big mogul owned Hollywood studios. The Mooney boys saw them all. T.V. was still an item beyond the pockets of most families. The cinema was pure escapism from the daily grind of working people's lives, and affordable. Looking back, those films, whether good and bad, were also unintentionally educational in that they opened our eyes to world history, world culture, the great cities of the globe and how people differed. The cinema also showed the dark world of criminality, and the good cops in pursuit of the villains.

One overriding feature of all those movies was the fact that good always overcomes bad. The 1950s was also a great period where Hollywood entered the world of science fiction with movies like War of the Worlds and It came from outer Space. So overall, the Mooney boys were not just being entertained but were being enlightened in ways that today's kids are not. We were so lucky to have had a mother who loved the cinema and never left her boys at home. It cost one shilling per adult and sixpence for kids. There were three categories of films. The 'U' certificate meant suitable for both adults and children, the 'A' certificate which meant children could watch if accompanied by an adult, and 'X' which signified adults only. Luckily for us brothers, 'X' films were few and far between. Foul language, explicit sex, and extreme violence in cinema did not arrive until almost twenty years later, so most adult themed films were given an 'A' certificate, which meant we were able to see most of the top films of that period. Alan Ladd as Shane, Robert Taylor in Quo Vadis, William Holden in Stalag 17, Humphrey Bogart and Katherine Hepburn in The African Queen, Marlon Brando in On the Waterfront, John Wayne in The Quiet Man, Marilyn Monroe in Niagara, Dirk Bogarde in Doctor in the House, James Stewart in Where the River Bends, Jack Hawkins in The Cruel Sea, and Norman Wisdom in Trouble in Store. So many wonderful diverse movies, all so different, but always entertaining. The funny thing was that because we usually had school the next day we would arrive at about six in the evening when the main feature was halfway through. That meant we would see the end and sit through the rest of the show till we reached the part where we went in. Such was the popularity of cinema, prior to every house having a television set, that programmes were continuous, running from early afternoon through till about 10.30.

There were two cinemas in Garston, and both were quite different. The Garston Empire is still standing as I write, though it has been closed for many years. It was a building that certainly was important to Garston people, for it had opened initially as a variety theatre, then its second life was as a cinema, and its final glory was as a Bingo Hall. It was very well run and had three changes of main feature each week. Sunday night was usually a film from the forties, and always of inferior quality. The CiscoKid, The Bowery Boys and Charlie Chan are three that come to mind. Monday to Wednesday, and Thursday through to Saturday evenings were the programmes of top-quality new releases. Those were the nights that us boys learned to love cinema. Those were the shows that introduced us to the best of Hollywood, and the best of British films. Movies became an interest that has lasted throughout each of our lives, and we are still movie buffs of that period.

We were in the Empire one night during the main feature, when a lovely black and white cat came up the aisle and settled on my knee. The Empire kept cats presumably to keep mice out of the cinema. You never saw them as a rule, but this one had obviously found a way in. I was seven years old, but the cat took a definite shine to me. Up until that time we had only had dogs, each of whom had come to sad endings, under lorry wheels or such. Knowing cats were so much easier to have as pets I persuaded my mam to hide it in her coat. It did not struggle all the way home and became a real and treasured member of the family for well over a decade. Strangely for an animal who was with us for so long, it was never given a name but remained as Cat until its death of old age in London in the sixties.

The Lyceum was hugely different from The Empire and was what was described at the time as a fleapit. Uncomfortable wooden seats and films that were old or were more in the B movie mould. Those I can remember were Lex Barker as Tarzan, and an ageing and rather potbellied Johnny Weissmuller as Jungle Jim. The 1950s was a period of cheaply made swashbuckling pirate films also, or adventure films set in ye old England, jungles, or in middle or far eastern countries. Of course, they were all made on the studio lots of Hollywood studios, with no thought given to reality. The actors, used primarily for their good looks, were contracted by the studios, and made a reasonable living by appearing in such twaddle. The British films shown were not of the J. Arthur Rank quality, but quickly made, mass produced comedies or dramas with long forgotten names like Ronald Shiner, Derek Farr, John Bentley, Donald Peers, Ronald Howard, Derek Bond, and Patrick Barr. Television was yet to make its mark in Britain, and the nation still had an insatiable appetite for what we termed 'the pictures.' Anyway, that was the kind of films shown at the Lyceum, but we still went! My mother had unintentionally given her boys a lifelong interest in American and British cinema. We were truly blessed.

There was another venue for kids to watch films in Garston. St Michael's had a large church hall called The Garston Institute at the top of King Street. On Saturday nights kids of all faiths and denominations paid 1 old penny for two hours of shorts. School forms were placed in rows. The programme never changed, first there was a selection of one-reel 1920s and 1930s comedies starring Charley Chase and Harold Lloyd, followed by the heroic deeds of Flash Gordon in his bid to save the universe from the dastardly exploits of the Emperor Ming. Each episode left kids wondering how Flash could survive falling off cliffs or being blown up with the immortal words 'Don't miss next week's thrilling episode!' Miraculously, he always escaped without a piece of his blond hair out of place and was always still around for next Saturday's performance.

CORONATION FEVER

In 1953, Shand Street, like the rest of Garston, pulled out all the stops for the Coronation of Princess Elizabeth. Outside the front door of most houses, trellis arches had been placed and decorated with paper roses. High above the whole street hung row after row off small Union Jack flags. Patriotism, not nationalism, still was important to people. The Union Jack, and loyalty to what it symbolised was still an important aspect in most people's lives. The war was still fresh, and after years of rationing and austerity the coronation of a young Queen gave an opportunity to come together, as they had not done since VE day. Not only was the coronation of a young princess a reason to feel proud, but the country was also taking pride in knowing that Mount Everest had been conquered for the first time by a British expedition.

Coming together returned to British people, just as it was in the war years. Parents seemed determined to make the occasion a special one for children, and Shand Street was no different. A street party for the kids took place on trestle tables, that I think were on loan from The Garston Tanning Company canteen. Food rationing was ending, so the tables were full of wonderful cakes and butties. The ladies of the street made themselves busy serving hot mugs of tea and sharing in the fun. It may be my imagination, but the tan yard may have also provided the large metal tea urns, cutlery, plates. At the top of Shand street was a quite modern house where the foreman of the tanning factory lived with his wife. I think she was involved in many such endeavours for the people of the street. Certainly, the tan yard was where the kids had a group photograph taken in the late afternoon. That was followed by a children only free ride around Liverpool on one of the green double decker Liverpool Council buses.

JOHN A, THE HONOURARY MUDMAN

No story of my childhood would be complete without telling of John A. I have not used his surname, as it is possible there are relatives still alive, or even John himself, and I have no wish to hurt anyone. It was the summer of 1954. School was over, and the long days of outdoor adventures had arrived. My mam was working in a factory in Speke, but it was a Saturday morning, and she was fortunate, in that she did not work at the weekends. For some reason I was the only brother at home, both John and Denis either down the shore, or up to innocent mischief elsewhere. I had a toy set of wooden various shaped bricks with which I was building a small house when a knock came at the front door. My mam was tidying up in the front room parlour, so I left it to her to answer the door. I heard a woman, who I knew my mother's name, asking if she could look after John for the day. My mam had asked both the lady and whoever was with her into the parlour. I had a few more blocks to finish my house, but my curiosity got the better of me, so I got up from the kitchen table, passed by the wooden stairs, and entered the parlour. There, seated next to a woman wearing too much bright red lipstick, was a very smartly dressed young boy who I concluded was slightly younger than myself. Little did I realise that this little boy would become one of the saddest stories of my childhood.

'Charlie has managed to get the weekend off and is coming up from London today and has asked me to meet him in Blackpool. It's his first break in months and he wants us to have the day together. I'll pick John up tonight; it's just for the day. He'll be no trouble; he's a quiet lad.'

I cannot remember how my mam reacted, but the outcome was that John was left with us for what my mam believed would be for the day.

I was to find out that Betty A had worked with my mother some time earlier in Speke. They were not particularly close friends, and so it was strange that she would know our address and come to ask my mam's assistance. Also strange was that her husband Charlie, who it turned out was a chef working in London, had not wanted to see his only child on such a brief visit. I've no idea if my mam questioned this, but the fact was I had a younger, cleanly dressed boy to look after. I looked him up and down and thought to myself he is too clean to play with me, and he is going to spoil my day. To be perfectly honest, I cannot recall how the day was spent, but what was obvious to me was that he was not a kid from 'under the bridge.' His voice was weak, his manners were perfect, and his clothes were spotless.

That evening John ate with us. My dad was always easy going and never questioned my mams decision to look after the boy for the day, and even tried to make the boy feel welcome. He was quiet, he was polite, but to me a bit too perfect. I did not say more to him than I had to and felt uncomfortable with another boy in my house. If the truth was known, I was probably a little bit jealous. The evening passed, but there was no sign of Betty A. Eight o'clock became nine o'clock, and when it got to 10.30 it was agreed that the boy's mother must have missed her train, and that young John should stay the night. It must be remembered that only the rich had telephones back then, so there would have been no way for her to make contact. By that time eldest brother Denis had his own bed, so I was going to share a bed with two John's! I did not like the prospect one bit, and was beginning to dislike this young boy who I did not know coming into my world. That night I tried to make him feel unwelcome by sticking my knees in his back or prodding him deliberately with my elbow. Much to my annoyance he never complained. In fact, he only ever spoke in answer to a question, and when he did speak it was always politely with a gentleness I just could not understand.

The next day came, and the next day went. Still, there was no sign of John's mother. My heart had cracked by the late afternoon, and I began to realise just how upset the poor young stranger was. Following a discussion with my dad, my mam comforted John and told him that he would accompany her to Heald Street Police Station in Garston Village. At that time, we were thinking that his mother must have had an accident, as no proper mother would leave her young son. The police had no report of Betty A. or anyone matching her description being hospitalised in Blackpool. The police officer showed little concern and intimated that John's mother was probably having a good time with her husband and had decided to stay longer. He told my mam that he could arrange for John to be put in care, but it was best to keep John and wait for his mother to turn up.

Well, that one night turned into the whole late summer of 1954. Betty A. never came back, and the police could only keep suggesting that John be put into care, or if agreeable, John stay where he was. There was no way my mam was going to put the lad in an institution, so John became another son to my parents, and a younger brother to me. We even started sharing my clothes! Gradually John began to be toughened up and initiated into the ways of 'under the bridge kids.' He learned how to laugh, lost his shyness, and genuinely seemed happy. He also learned how to swim in Garston baths, along with the fun of getting muddy feet and dirty kneecaps down the shore. He learned to accept cuts and bruises without crying, but most of all, he learned how to be an 'under the bridge' kid! Where we went, John went. I was still the youngest, and still prone to being jealous. When he started calling my dad 'Father Fleck,' a nickname only used by his sons, I remember rebuking him; 'He's not your father Fleck, he's my dad.' I can also remember getting upset and shouting at him when he slipped up and called my mother mam, 'She's not your mam, she's, my mam!'

He gradually learned not to make such slip ups, and my mother became Aunty Vi. He still called my dad Father Fleck, but I learned to live with that one because John had by that time been accepted as a member of the family.

Suddenly it was September. Within days, school would replace the days of constant adventure down the shore. My mam had been talking of enrolling John into Banks Road School along with my brother John and myself. She had never given up checking with the police, but they said they had been unable to trace either of John's parents, and that it was best he stays where he was. 1954 was a vastly different world when it came to the welfare of children. The major problem seemed to be that there were just too many children to care for. A postwar baby boom had occurred, and school classrooms were bulging. Children's homes dealt with the same problem of overcrowding. Orphan children, and those from broken homes were systematically being shipped out on ships to Australia and Canada by the likes of Dr Barnardo's and the Roman Catholic Church.

It was late one Saturday morning that I answered a loud knock on the front door. In front of me stood a face I will never forget. It was a man with thinning reddish hair and loose-fitting false teeth. It was Charlie A, John's father. From the moment I met him I knew that he was not a good man. John seemed elated to see him however, and within minutes my young friend was being led up Shand Street by the father who had abandoned him.

I did not know what to do. I was not yet eight years old, my dad was working, and my mam was out. Brothers John and Denis were probably down the shore, so I had no one to turn to. I was confused and in no position to stop a grown man from collecting his son. I remember wishing my dad had been there as I knew he would have rearranged Charlie A's false teeth! I decided to follow them for as long as I could and see where they went. I ran up King Street as fast as my seven-year-old legs would take me, and there was John. The joy had gone from his face, and he had returned to being the placid little boy again. The father who had not seen his own son for months had sat him outside The Blackburne Arms whilst he went inside for a beer. I pleaded with John to come back home with me. I told him his Aunty Vi and Father Fleck would be upset, as would John and Denis. I told him that he could not just go off without a word to anyone. It was no use, his dad had come for him, and he had to do what he was told. He was clearly upset, and I was confused and not knowing what to do. Finally, I told him I was going under the bridge, in the hope of meeting my mam at the bus stop. I pleaded with him not to go off, to make some excuse, but to just to wait for Aunty Vi. I never saw him again.

For weeks, my mam was constantly returning to the police station for any news. The attitude she was met with was that John was back with his legal father, and the matter was closed. They did however promise to let her know if any reports of John's whereabouts became known. She was determined to know that John was safe. It went quiet then, and slowly things returned to the way they were before John came into our lives. My mam never gave up, questioning anyone she felt might have known either parent, but nothing.

We learned many months later from the police that John had been put into care, then along with hundreds of other needy children been put on a ship and transported to a new life in Australia. We found out that he had been neglected by his father, and neighbours had reported the lad's plight to the police. As for his mother we never found out where she had disappeared, but we heard she did turn up in Liverpool some years later. I have a theory however, but not one I can ever prove. I do not think Betty A. ever went to Blackpool. In my mind she went off to London to be with that scoundrel of a husband she was besotted with. I think that they probably shared a summer of bliss, with too much drink, and too much living on the edge. Then, when the money ran out, reality crept in, and Mr and Mrs A. had a massive fall out. The man was a no-good shiftless character, and he had probably lost his job. Returning to Liverpool, he likely used his son to get his wife back. Such people do exist, and kids like John were the innocent ones who paid the price. I have no idea what kind of a life John had. There have been reports of ill treatment towards many of the children sent to Australia. Some were used as virtual slaves by unscrupulous families, and many cases of sexual abuse. Of course, there were also many lucky enough to have been placed in good homes. If he made it through, my wish is that he was one of the fortunate ones. He certainly deserved better than to have had the parents he had. One thing I am certain of, he would never have forgotten the summer of 1954 when he got dirty kneecaps and became a proper 'under the bridge' kid of Garston, nor would he ever have forgotten the acceptance and affection shown to him by the two people he called Aunty Vi and Father Fleck.

THE RAGMAN COMETH

Work horses were still very much used in early 1950s Liverpool. Even the Liverpool Corporation used them for the weekly collection of rubbish. A much smaller horse was used by the regular visit from the ragman, whose visits were always welcomed by the kids. Quite wisely, our ragman did not give out daft things like balloons. No, he brought something far more interesting that he knew would really grab the kid's attention. He gave out authentic Real McCoy American comics. Difficult to describe, but a whole industry has now sprung up in Hollywood recreating the Marvel characters from those comics. The comics we enjoyed from the ragman were most the horror ones like Tales from the Crypt and Black Magic. The graphics on all the comics were amazing, but the horror comics were really, very creepy. Lads were so desperate to get the comics they were going upstairs and taking the blankets off the beds.

A WALL OF SNOW

The winter of 1954 had started off quite mildly but rapidly changed during the beginning of 1955. It was always great when Shand Street kids woke up to a snow laden street, especially if the snow fell at the beginning of the weekend. That is what occurred on a Friday evening in early January. It did not take long for the kids to get themselves outside on Saturday morning. I cannot remember how it started but someone started down one end of the street rolling his snowball, slowly it became bigger and bigger. Soon everyone cottoned on, and all the kids were rolling their snowballs up the street making them bigger and bigger. As the morning progressed a wall of snow and ice built up at the entrance to the street. By mid-day, the wall was three feet in height. We had left an entrance on the pavement for our elders to come and go. The thing I remember most was that no adult ever complained. I think if the kids of today something like that some adult did would be on the phone to the police.

GARSTON, CHRISTMAS PAST

It is possible that I am being cynical, but Christmas seemed a lot more special for 1950s kids. Times were still hard, and England was not the multicultural country it has become. Schools placed much more emphasis on Christianity, and the true significance of the religious holiday. We knew all about Bethlehem, no room at the inn, and the humble birth of Jesus in a manger. To us it was a magical story, and one we just took as fact. We also thought of Christmas as a musical time with lots of carols, which were never maudlin, but were melodic and in the eyes of a little boy quite beautiful. My favourite was always Silent Night. I liked singing back then, and it did not do me any harm in later life. We would of course get up early in anticipation of what was hanging on the end of the bed. Of course, we had hung our long grey socks up the previous night. There would be an orange, nuts, some sweets, and sometimes a packet of dates. It seldom varied, but it was Christmas, a special time, and there was always a special present to be had. Because I was a movie fan l normally got an annual book on Hollywood stars. It would be full of articles on the stars of the time. Those I can recall were Jeff Chandler, Rock Hudson, and Doris Day. I loved reading about where those stars lived, and all the glamour associated with them. The annuals were books that came out specifically for Christmas. Like most boys back then, I loved anything to do with the Wild West. Western movies were at their peak, and I remember my dad telling us that John Wayne was box office star of the year. The Buffalo Bill Annual was another Christmas favourite because it told tales of the characters of the old west. It was beautifully illustrated and gave me knowledge of such characters as Wyatt Earp and Doc Holliday, Frank and Jesse James, Billy the Kid and Pat Garret, and Wild Bill Hickock, with informative narratives of their lives, and deaths.

One Christmas my mam won a Christmas draw. The first prize was a goose. It had to be collected from around Smithdown Road. That meant it had to be transported on Christmas Eve on the bus. The snag was that it was huge and looked more like an ostrich. It caused a bit of a laugh on the bus but somehow, we got it home. It would have been too big for the oven, so I think my mam had to cut it up and cook it in segments. I can remember all the fatty juices she had to keep removing. It was worth all the hassle. I can still taste that succulent meat, and I don't think I've tasted goose since. Another recollection of Christmas was a visit to Blackler's for the meeting with a very bad breathed, and cotton wooled Father Christmas in the grotto.

Those then were just some of my memories and

recollections of Garston, but what of the man who drove up our street in the black Jaguar? The uncle who encouraged us to leave behind all we knew? Well Bryan Mooney had a story that is well worth telling. He was without question the prodigal son, the black sheep. So different from his father, and yet strangely similar. Both were driven by an adrenaline that few of us have, and a need for exhilaration. Uncle Bryan's problem was the way he chose to fulfil that need, and the terrible consequences this would bring for his daughter.

THE BLACK SHEEP SON

'Brian was a little rascal,' a simple description of my Uncle Bryan told to me by an elderly lady in a care home in Skelmersdale in 1991. I visited her after she had answered an ad I had placed in the Old Pals section of the Liverpool Echo regarding the Mooney family of Finchley Road, Anfield. She had been a neighbour and had grown up near the Mooney's during the 1920s through to the end of the war. She had spoken of her fondness for the family, and said they were well liked by all. However, she did say that Bryan was different to his siblings. He was hyper and prone to do daft things without thought of consequence. He also chose his friends less carefully and got himself involved in silly minor misdemeanours. Whereas his brothers became heavily involved in sports of all kinds, as Bryan grew, he had an attribute that his father found perplexing. He was musical! I suppose with the Irish and Scottish blood running in his veins it was not too surprising, but it went against the grain to what Denis Mooney wanted of his sons!

Bryan was to eventually become proficient on mandolin, guitar, and ukulele. To gain any form of ability on such instruments meant learning from others. Liverpool being the cosmopolitan city it was, was full of music. Bryan's musical tastes needed to be broadened, and that meant mixing with people from diverse cultures. Bryan had no qualms about friendship with men of colour, for they were the key to a world he desperately wanted to join.

The 1930's was a remarkable decade for popular music, and Bryan Mooney gloried in every aspect of it. Being young he would have taken in the hits of the time like Dinah, All of Me, Night and Day, Try A Little Tenderness, Sweet Georgia Brown, Chinatown, and Smoke Gets in Your Eyes. His mixing with diverse raced musicians gained him a wider knowledge of world music.

One tale my mam told me, presumably told to her by my dad was of the day Bryan was caught busking. My grandparents, like most couples of the early 1930s, loved the cinema. After leaving an afternoon matinee at Gaumont Palace, my grandfather had seen Bryan with a group of mixed-race boys busking for money to the people queuing for the next show. He became rigid and did not speak to my grandmother on the way home. Once home he expressed his anger at seeing his son busking for money. My grandmother would have tried to pacify him, but his Edwardian stiffness and displeasure was palpable. Whatever was said to his son fell on deaf ears, for Bryan saw nothing wrong and carried on as before. Bryan was improving his musical prowess, and if it met with disapproval, so be it.

He learned of the man they called 'The Singing Brakeman'. Jimmie Rodgers had worked on the railways of America during the wild times of prohibition, so his bluesy songs always had a tale to tell. By the 1920s and 30s wax records had become a worldwide phenomenon and Jimmie Rodgers, who often yodelled in his songs, was popular with people of all races. In fact, there was a very black influence in his songs, yet today, Rodgers is credited as being 'the father of country music'. His songs were often taken from his own experiences, and they drew pictures of railroad hobos, lost love, hard times, bar room brawls, gun toting bad men, and fast women. Even today songs like 'Frankie and Johnnie' are still popular in the jazz fraternity. Uncle Bryan would have loved the Rodgers lyrics, all of which brought visions of an untamed America, its colourful characters, and its excitement.

As Bryan became more proficient, his knowledge of music grew, and he became aware and overawed by a French guitarist named Django Reinhardt. The gypsy Parisienne records introduced Bryan to a unique form of guitar playing, and jazz. His quick-change chords were made all the more remarkable since Reinhardt only had two fingers and a stump on his left hand, having lost the others in a fire! Listening, watching, and trying to emulate the 'tricks and licks' of every style brought Bryan great satisfaction, my grandfather would have been less impressed and would have considered his son to have been wasting his life. A decision was made that saw Bryan Mooney, aged18, enrolling into the prestigious Scots Guards! According to my mam it was my grandfather that got his son enrolled. Years later Uncle Bryan told me he had joined of his own volition, and without pressure from anyone. Being tall, upright, fit, and extremely smart, his acceptance into the guards was a foregone conclusion.

The year must have been 1935 and he seems to have been an enthusiastic and model soldier. Like his father before him, he represented his country in Palestine, which was a British protectorate. His unit were acting as policemen, whose thankless duty was to keep the peace between the native Arabs and the increasing number of Jews who were arriving from Europe. Seen as the enemy by both sides, it was a no-win situation for the British army. I do not know how long uncle Bryan spent in Palestine, but he was there in December 1936, a time of great unrest and violence between Arab and Jew.

Later he found himself back in London dressed in the traditional uniform of his regiment. Resplendent with his bearskin busby hat, he found himself marching with total precision outside the great palaces of the new King. Being in England's capital, and being musical, there was only one place for a young off duty soldier to go. Soho was a bohemian open door to foreign culture, with street markets, music, gambling, nightclubs, artists, street entertainers, theatres, foreign restaurants, vice, and criminals. Being young and inquisitive, and finally being his own man, my uncle found himself fascinated by the area. I would imagine he had friends within the guards who went with him, but he certainly spent a lot of his free time there. Bryan had also found it a great place to sit in and 'jam' with musicians of many nationalities.

There was another element in Soho that Bryan found a fascination for, and that was the criminal fraternity. Although he had been raised in a household where criminality was seen as obnoxious, Bryan Mooney was impressed. He was fascinated and felt comfortable being around such colourful characters who lived outside the law.

This was my mother's story of the one deciding incident that made Bryan Mooney turn his back on the norms of society. As stated earlier, Uncle Bryan had been mischievous, prone to do things without thinking of the consequences. On returning to his barracks one night the driver of an open top sports car had left his pair of leather gloves on the dashboard. Uncle Bryan was later charged with stealing them, something he vehemently denied all his life. It is highly possible that the gloves, and car belonged to an officer. How he was found to be the perpetrator of the theft I have no idea. The Scot's Guards was an elite unit with a strict code of honour. Uncle Bryan was charged with theft, brought before his superiors, and discharged.

With no desire to face his disgrace back in Liverpool, my uncle decided to lose himself. Like most people, he was well aware that a war was coming and that his country would once again need him. However, he was bitter and angry at his dismissal for a crime he always swore he had not committed. His opinion became 'if they want me, they'll bloody well have to come and find me!' I do not know if Uncle Bryan had been involved in engineering prior to his army enrolment but he was soon working in The Rootes Motor Company in Coventry.

GUNS OR GUITARS?

War was declared in September 1939 and the army eventually did find him, and like other young men of his age, he was kitted out in a khaki uniform! Bryan had changed, especially to those in authority. He was bitter and had altered his views on the military completely. He would do his stint because he had to, but he would do so under duress, and he was not going to be a hero for anyone. He seems to have had contacts within the army system and wangled himself into an ENSA unit. Such units travelled to just behind battle lines where they kept up the troops morale by playing musical revues, and entertaining. So, his war years were spent not with a gun in his hand, but with a musical stringed instrument! Unfortunately, I have no knowledge of where his unit went but suffice to say it was a cushy number.

Once demobbed in 1945 he remained in London. From the moment he put on his civvy clothes he knew he was going to live according to his own code and take orders from no one. Bryan Mooney, the ex-Guardsman, was gone, and a new and unrecognisable Bryan Mooney was about to emerge.

THE NEED FOR EXCITEMENT

There was money to be made in a post war London, and he was going to get his share. He had acquaintances in Soho, and with post war shortages, Bryan Mooney went for what he thought was the more lucrative and exciting way to earn a crust! Somewhere during those years after the war, he had married. It is all a bit of a mystery, but here is the little bit l know. His wife was Irish, they lived in the Tufnell Park area and had a son appropriately named Brian, with an I, not a Y. He told my eldest brother Denis many years later that he had married in Ireland in a huge church. That is all l know of the woman, apart from a few black and white photos l have of the two of them, taken in the late 40's or early 50's. Photos in which Bryan is dressed in tailored suits, looking every inch of what he had become, a well-dressed criminal. Not surprisingly any kind of normality quickly faded in the marriage and within a few years they had parted. I would not be surprised if Uncle Bryan had done some time behind bars, possibly such an event caused them to split? I have no idea. Having married an Irish catholic however, divorce would never have been an option.

I know little of my uncle's London life between the end of the war and the morning he turned up on our doorstep in 1955. The few things I do know is that it was a very lucrative period for the black market and for those shady characters who seemed able to magically produce the goods that people wanted or were in short supply of.

Everything was cash in the late 40s and early 50s, and wage snatches could be very lucrative for the criminal fraternity. Freight lorry hold ups were another popular way of getting goods to sell on the black market. Nothing was ever openly discussed, but my uncle always had the best cars, always dressed beautifully, rented out three large houses in North London, had acquired a beautiful German partner, fathered a little girl, had lots of dubious friends, and never did one ounce of work!

We arrived in London less than a month after my uncle had first shown up in Garston. I remember the mixture of excitement and anxiety during the train journey from Lime Street. I recall my mother crying on the train, obviously worrying about the decisions she and my dad had quickly taken, and the strain she had obviously gone through. Not yet nine years old, it was unsettling for me to see her so upset.

We were met at Euston by my uncle, the steam train having taken what must have been at least six hours. Being driven in his Jaguar through the streets of London was very memorable. I vividly recall seeing the huge placards advertising London theatre shows, and my first viewing of a red London bus. What soon became obvious, even to a little boy, was that London had taken more than its fair share of German bombs. There were few areas without gaps between the buildings, that had created overgrown and weeded craters. Eventually we pulled into a road of Edwardian three story houses. I was impressed. My expectations rose.

On entering the house where our new abode was to be, those expectations quickly eroded! The hallway had linoleum covered floors, and there was no shade on the low wattage main hall light. Our little house in Garston didn't have much, but this place was certainly no step up the ladder. The flat had the darkest grimmest wallpaper and consisted of three rooms. Making things worse was the knowledge that we shared a toilet and bathroom with other tenants who lived both above and below us. This was not the London l had envisioned or seen in the movies at the Empire, Garston. I did not like it, and my brothers did not like it. We wanted to go back, but in deference to our parents made little comment. That feeling of being removed to another, and more indifferent environment never really left us.

The reality was that we were in no position to argue, Denis was just thirteen, with a two-year gap between both John and me. Eventually we were moved to another one of the houses Bryan rented in the same street. The rooms were bigger, but prior to a division being made to add a room, we had moved from 3 rooms to two. Even now over half a century later it is a period I have largely erased from my mind. With my alien Liverpool accent, I had a hard time at school; I felt lost and never really adjusted. I did my best as I knew my parents loved the fact that they were now somewhere where there was always employment. Though there was much to see and do, my brothers and I would always feel alien.

We were eventually introduced to my uncle's partner (we kids were told it was his wife). German by birth, her name was Helen, and she was very beautiful. She was a good 15 years younger than Bryan but had given him a little girl (also named Helen), two years before. For some reason they chose to call her 'Girlie'. We were visiting them in their very well furnished flat at the top of one of Bryan's other properties. Though quite pleasant, there was a worldliness to Helen that made me feel ill at ease. She was German, but there was not one trace of an accent. Years later I would learn about the allied bombing in the summer of 1943 of her native Hamburg, with the use of phosphoric bombs. I came to realise just how traumatic and horrific her formative years must have been. She would have been the ideal German Aryan child. Like all children under the Nazi regime, she would have been brainwashed at school into believing that she was part of the master race. Such events and unimaginable scenes that killed thousands would harden anyone, especially a young beautiful girl. My mam would learn later that she had married an English soldier to get out of Germany, then once in England had left him. She could be very likeable, but she had a definite hardness. I also found her to be too strict with Girlie, who was a typical boisterous two-year-old child, with the fine features of both parents. Their flat was filled with very tasteful furniture, but it was the numerous stringed musical instruments hanging on the walls that caught my eye. Not only were there guitars and mandolins, but there were also strange east European instruments that 1 would still find it difficult to name. At that time, I knew nothing of Bryan's musical ability, but was intrigued. I most certainly did not realise just how much of an influence those instruments, and my newfound uncle would have on my future life.

The months passed, and to give my parents credit, they took their boys to all the city's wonderful array of museums, sights, markets, and parks. Such days out were great, and I know that both parents worked hard to integrate us into the city.

As time drew on my parents became more aware of Bryan's criminal activities.

It was not openly discussed, but it became obvious that

my dad disapproved of his younger brother. Looking back, I think it became a question of toleration, and a preference not to know. My mother always knew a great deal more and became a good listener to Helen. London offered my dad the opportunity of doing non manual work. He was a man who had received an excellent education, was good at maths, and had a handwriting ability that was sheer perfection. Within a short period, he was working in a suit, collar and tie, doing the office work Liverpool denied him. My mother also found work easy to acquire in the catering industry So as the months turned into years our little family settled into London life, but Liverpool never went away. Uncle Bryan remained something of a mystery man.

MY MUSICAL MENTOR

Maybe it was only because l was able to be a companion for Girlie, but a lot of my school holidays in those early London years were spent at Bryan's. His was a place of music, with records constantly being played. He had a wonderful piece of furniture that was a television, a record player, and a radio combined. Often the instruments would come down off the wall and he would show me his ability on the guitar and mandolin. It is possible he knew that l had that ' musical something.' and that he was trying to bring it out. That 'musical something', whatever it was, came to fruition in 1957 when my eldest brother Denis, who had just started work, bought a guitar.

An American form of music had taken England by storm. Kids all over the country were forming small groups to play what had become known as skiffle. Former banjo player and singer for The Chris Barber Jazz band, Lonnie Donegan (who Uncle Brian knew, and played guitar with), had taken the British record charts by storm with an American folk/blues song called 'Rock Island Line'. Lonnie played guitar and it soon became obvious that the traditional songs he was enjoying big hits with, were easy three chord numbers. Every teenage lad in the country seemed to be acquiring guitars, including young schoolboys like Eric Clapton,

Hank Marvin, Joe Brown, John Lennon, Paul McCartney, and George Harrison. The guitars were complimented by homemade double basses made from tea chests, a broom handle, and a piece of taut string. The last instrument in a skiffle group that provided the percussion would be a metal washboard. By tapping the rungs of the utensil with sewing thimbles a steady rhythm was kept. Skiffle groups were popping up everywhere, in every city and town.

A new system of purchasing had been introduced called hire purchase. It meant goods could be purchased on a weekly payment scheme. This suited Denis, who with my mother's signature bought a German made guitar. Only just a little over a decade since the end of the war, the choice for available guitars was limited. The most affordable models were made in Germany, and though they looked good, the strings were high off the neck, making it exceedingly difficult to get a clear ringing sound. Pressing down and getting a sweet clear note on the strings could only be achieved by making the skin on the end of the fingers hard! This entailed lots of dedicated practice and a lot of pain. Within a month Denis said it hurt his fingers too much, had grown tired of it, and put it in the corner. My mother noticed that l had started to pick it up, and encouraged me to practice, 'You learn it properly and l will take over the payments from Denis,' she said. I had by that time struggled through my first song. It was a two-chord sea shanty I had found in The Bert Weedon Book of Chords called Bobby Shaftoe. I took up my mother's challenge and picked the guitar up every spare minute I could find. I practised my chords, getting the ends of my fingers hard. 1 listened to anything and everything and tried to emulate the little instrumental bits of records, or from the TV commercials. That German guitar brought me a great deal of pleasure during my school years, and I never realised that one day I would earn money by playing. Of course, Uncle Bryan was pleased that he now had a nephew who was learning the guitar and was interested in music. Becoming proficient however was not easy, and it took me several years. I never was able to reach the standard of Bryan, but that was because he had met and been encouraged by other more learned musicians, whereas the only one I ever met was the kid in the mirror.

DUBIOUS FRIENDS AND FLASHY CARS

Throughout those early years in London I would spend most of my school holidays with Uncle Bryan and Girlie. Helen sometimes went out to work, not because she needed the money, but because she liked the independence that work gave her. My days with Bryan were normally spent driving to all parts of London visiting people that Bryan knew. "I've just got to see a geezer" he would say as he left me in the back of his latest car with Girlie. I knew even at that age what my uncle and his cronies were discussing. Sometimes I would catch a glimpse of his 'friends'. They were shady characters, but I knew not to ask questions. l just felt it was none of my business. My dad was an honest man, and while it was nice to drive around in posh cars it never entered my head to be envious of Bryan's lifestyle. I was always more comfortable with the little we had back home.

There is no doubt in my mind that Uncle Bryan loved Girlie very much, but his way of life always came first. Cars played a big part, and they were always models that fitted the image he liked to purvey. I remember him saying that his brand-new Ford Zephyr was one of the first to come off the ramps at their Dagenham factory. Such late 1950s Ford cars were big, flashy, and very American in style. This was before the opening of motorways, and l have one memory of Bryan showing off and opening his new Zephyr on the north circular road and reaching a speed of 120 m.p.h.

HIJACKS AND GELIGNITE

As mentioned previously, this was a time before motorways. Long distance lorry drivers would have to take their lorries on quiet back country lanes, perfect places to do highway robberies, especially if the driver was 'in on the job'. Bryan got a lot of inside information from the drivers themselves. During the 1950's a good portion of heavy road transportation was carried out by British Road Services, a nationalised company. It is hardly surprising that their main depot was within walking distance of Uncle Bryan's flat, and that he had several of the company's drivers as 'acquaintances'. Goods carried could be cigarettes, alcohol, jewellery, or even fur coats. Those huge lorries could be full of tens of thousands of pounds worth of goods. The art was to know when such valuables were being transported and discussing the best and quietest place to unload. The driver would obviously have to take a bit of roughing up to make them look innocent, but he would be well recompensed for his bruises later. I have learned in later years that there were bank jobs, not with the use of shotguns, but by means of tunnelling and gelignite.

I would never say that Bryan and his cronies were anything other than rogues, but l cannot help having a slight admiration for their sheer bravado and planning ability. My impression was that these were flawed characters on the edge of society who needed that bit of excitement and challenge. That it came from crime is however unfortunate. I must admit that most of my uncle's lower echelon 'acquaintances' were polite, seldom swore, or behaved in anything other than a correct manner towards either Girlie or the young boy that I was. One 'friend' was a guy called Johnny, who (between jobs) Bryan used to do the maintenance on his properties. He was always friendly and well mannered, and he had kids of his own.

Another 'friend' of Bryan moved into the flat beneath ours with his wife. He was affable, and seemed personable, and always said hello. I can't remember too much of his wife, but she seemed nice enough, but I did not take too much notice. They had not been living there long when a commotion broke out. My folks were at work, and I was on my own, probably during a school holiday. I heard Bryan hurriedly going into the flat downstairs and several minutes later the wife was screaming hysterically. Concerned, but not wanting to interfere, I went out in the hallway where I could not help but hear my uncle trying to pacify the hysterical woman. I could hear him saying things like "he wouldn't have felt any pain," which only made the woman scream and sob louder. The drama went on for at least an hour, with other 'acquaintances' of Bryan coming and going. From what I could make out, they were trying to calm her down because her husband had been involved in some kind of accident. By the time the fracas concluded there were several more 'friends' coming and going. The crying woman was led to one of the cars. Bryan's acquaintances carried out several bags and several suitcases, which I presumed were the couple's possessions. Once loaded up, the cars left, and I never saw either the husband or the wife again. Later I told my mam, but not my dad. By this time, my dad avoided and had a total dislike of his younger brother, and I thought it best to say nothing.

Strangely, with his left-wing views, my dad bought the Daily Express every day. I was probably only twelve, but I always read his newspaper. Looking through, I read a report of a catastrophe that had taken place in an army depot outside London. There had been a huge explosion of gelignite in an area that was strictly out of bounds and under constant high security watch. The sparse remnants of a male body had been found. I may have been only twelve years old, but I was never stupid. I put two and two together. The body parts they found belonged to Bryan's friend from the flat below, of that I am certain. To rob a big safe, required gelignite, and gelignite was not on sale in the corner shop, it had to be stolen, and the army would be one certain place that held such dangerous material. I thought it best to let the matter be forgotten. Just another one of Bryan's little escapades that were better left unquestioned.

THE MUSICAL THIEF

Uncle Bryan and his 'cohorts' were relatively safe in the London area. Envelopes could change hands between the criminal and the cops in certain back street pubs. I witnessed this exchange many times in later years but never questioned. Thick envelopes would be passed quickly from Bryan's inner jacket pocket. These plain clothes coppers did not socialise, and little was ever said, but it was obvious to me that a proportion of London detectives back then were as bent as the criminals.

Throughout all those years uncle Bryan kept up his music. His back garden was often used for sessions with friends, especially in the summer. There was one musical session when there were at least eight musicians playing Hawaiian music, and they were all Polynesians! It was a wonderful way for a young boy to spend an afternoon. There were Hawaiian guitars, mandolins, ukuleles and acoustic guitars, and singing. Some evenings uncle Bryan and Helen would drive to Wapping by the river. Their destination was one of London's oldest pubs The Prospect of Whitby. In the 1950's it was a meeting place for musicians, especially guitarists. I was too young to go, but it was the kind of venue that my uncle and Helen would have taken my parents on our initial arrival in London.

BRIAN MOONEY

As well as musical get togethers, the back garden of 33 Pemberton Gardens had another purpose that was witnessed by the next-door neighbour and friend of Girlie. Through the wonders of Facebook, she had contacted my niece and told of the following recollection. Apparently when she was a young girl, she heard a lot of banging going on in my uncle's garden. Several burly men with hammers were assisting my uncle in their quest to open a small safe that had somehow come into their possession.

PRISON AND ENCROACHING OLD AGE

The years passed; I had become a teenager, and Girlie was too big and pretty to need a minder. I saw less and less of my uncle and Girlie, for I had become a teenager, and the swinging sixties had arrived. London was certainly waking up from its post war slumber. I had discovered girls, and I wanted to enjoy my teenage years. Strangely enough, most of my friends never knew I played guitar. It was just something I did at home, or on trips back to Liverpool. It was bound to happen that Bryan's good luck would end, and that the good times were beginning to reach a conclusion. This occurred because he became less cautious and did jobs outside of London. That meant that when the cops came calling, he was unable to deploy one of his infamous envelopes. He was a marked man from then on, and a frequent guest of Her Majesty.

On all the occasions of my uncles going into the 'slammer' Helen was dutiful and visited him regularly. However, she was still a very beautiful woman and one of Bryan's dubious acquaintances was starting to take more than an interest in her. He obviously did not believe in the old term ' honour amongst thieves' and was soon being 'dishonourable' with Helen! I had met the gentleman in question on a few occasions, and did not like him one bit. Like those other Cockney miscreants the Krays, he had a dangerous self-assurance and swagger that l found frightening and obnoxious. To put it more simply, he had a big mouth, swore openly, and was detestable. (Some years later Bryan told my eldest brother Denis that he could have had him bumped off for five hundred quid). I am in no doubt Bryan knew such people.

Girlie was in her mid-teens, her father was in and out of prison, and her mother was openly cavorting with her new lover and spending less and less time at home. This left Girlie open to mixing with the wrong types. She had by this time left school and got a job in a local fashion shop. She was a lovely girl and had looked the epitome of the 60's, fashionable, mini skirted and very pretty, girl about town.

Being a teenager myself, l needed to go my own way, so aged 19 I did what some of my Liverpool mates did each year and went to work in Jersey for a summer season. I had gone because I was not happy in London, and needed to enjoy my youth, have some sun and be independent. Unexpected things happen in life, and that island introduced me to the love of my life. Without going into detail, I fell for a girl I knew was the one before I was 20 years old. 1966, the year England won the World Cup, and the Beatles gave the world songs like 'Eleanor Rigby', turned out to be the most important year of my life. June, my future wife returned to teachers training college in Newcastle in the September, and I returned to London. I had little to do with Bryan, mainly because he was often behind bars somewhere. My priorities lay elsewhere, and I had become engrossed in working and saving enough money to return permanently to Jersey and marry. My life was solely fixated on thoughts other than Uncle Bryan or Girlie.

It took me two years to save enough, so in 1969 I left London for good and got married one year later. My life in London was over and all my thoughts and efforts were concentrated on securing a stable lifetime in Jersey.

Sadly, my father-in-law died a year after our marriage in 1971.It had therefore become a ritual to spend our Sunday lunchtime at our home with Eileen, June's mother. One Sunday lunchtime two years after we had married, Eileen mentioned an article she was reading in The Sunday People newspaper concerning a 19-year-old girl named Helen Mooney. She asked me if Helen was a relative. Having passed me the newspaper l read a headline that broke my heart.

THE SUNDAY PEOPLE

JUNE 1972
'We broke the heroin gang, but we couldn't save 19-year-old Helen's life'.

I could not believe what I was reading. Girlie was dead. Not only was she dead, but she had been a heroin addict. I could not take it in. My hand was shaking as I began reading a horror story. Girlie, the pretty girl who had everything to live for, had for a prolonged period been talking to Frank Thorne, one of the newspapers top investigative reporters. Mr Thorne told how he had gotten to know Helen (Girlie) in the Knightsbridge tube station. He had posed initially as a hippie and enquired about purchasing heroin from her. During the time he got to know her she told him that she was an addict, and was being used, along with other girls to approach punters in the station. Her reward was not money, but packets of the obnoxious powder she was selling. She also told him that she knew she would soon be dead. Here are some of the words Mr Thorne had written over fifty years ago:

> I walked behind her coffin as it was carried into the church adjoining Pemberton Gardens, Holloway, London where Helen lived. I sent a wreath for her funeral and wondered how many more bright teenagers like Helen would have to

die before this vicious drug trafficking is stopped. I mourned the girl whose short life began to ebb away four years ago when she innocently began experimenting with pills. Helen Mooney's traumatic teenage years carry a grim warning to parents and teenagers alike. Helen progressed from pills to heroin and became a registered addict. She joined a gang of five girl pushers operating mainly from stations on the Piccadilly line. She told me, 'You know when you take heroin you are killing yourself, but you just don't think about it.'

Helen was found dead in the squalor of her own bedroom. She had been living rough for several weeks. Pills were scattered about the room. Her father Bryan Mooney is serving a six-month prison sentence for handling stolen goods. He was allowed home for the funeral. He told me, 'She was a slave to heroin and the people who exploited her addiction.'

'I had no idea what was going on until it was too late.'

Helen's death has shattered Mr Mooney. He and his wife parted some years ago, and Helen was his world. During the funeral service I thought back to that day when I sat with Helen on Knightsbridge tube station. I watched a stream of pathetic young addicts come and go and saw Helen take £60 from them in 15 minutes. The tube gang was smashed when The Sunday People exposed the racket. They split up and Helen agreed to go into a London hospital in an effort to 'kick' her addiction. The cure was short lived. When she came out her father was in prison. Helen returned home alone.

It was neighbour Wilf Newton who found Helen's twisted contorted body on that fatal morning, 'I shall never forget the sight of her in that bedroom. She must have been in terrible pain when she died. Her poor body was deformed and twisted as if all her muscles had contracted in different directions.'

'The people who gave her these drugs should have seen her the way I saw her. They would have seen her face for the rest of their lives.'

Mr Newton's wife Brenda said tearfully, 'It was like losing one of our own. Helen was such a nice kid. We had known her for nine years and tried to help her all we could.'

Then Mr Newton gave what could be Helen's epitaph. 'Helen often told us she wished she were dead. Well, she has got her wish, poor kid. She didn't have a chance.'

I felt guilty that I was in complete ignorance of poor Girlie's life. I phoned my mother, and she too knew nothing as any contact had virtually broken down long before. Girlie's mother had run off with her fancy man, and my dad had long since given up on his brother. Through the horror of Girlie's terrible death there was one thing that shone through the article. Both the reporter and the neighbours were not just moved by Girlie, but they genuinely liked and were emotionally moved by her. She could have grown to be happily married and had children and possibly been a grandmother. Her life ended because of parents who put themselves before their child. I am in no doubt that her death broke Bryan. Girlie's mother had left him, and his daughter was dead aged 19. Yes, he was a broken man, but as far as I was concerned, rightly so. His life of crime, his choice of friends, his continual misdeeds had all caught up with him. If ever there was a case of crime does not pay, it applied to my Uncle Bryan.

Girlie's mother Helen was never seen again. At the time I held a lot of contempt for the woman who never even went to her daughter's funeral. Over the years, however, my feelings have softened. She too had been robbed of her childhood and had been a brainwashed child of the Nazi system. In 1943, when she should have been enjoying her teenage years, she was witness to the terrible retribution of the R.A.F. Phosphorus bombs rained down on her native Hamburg causing the city to erupt in flames and causing the deaths of thousands. What she saw and survived would have mentally scarred any young girl for life. She was a damaged person and had built a hard shell around herself where open feelings were hidden. I am sure, however, that she suffered many sleepless nights in the years that followed. She will be long dead now, so it really does not matter.

RETRIBUTION FOR A LONELY OLD MAN

On his release from prison Bryon Mooney's world was empty. His beautiful partner, and his daughter were gone. His way of life was all but gone too. Many of his friends had passed away, were guests of her majesty, or with sufficient ill-gotten gains were able to retire. Age was catching up with him, and he found himself alone, representing an almost extinct breed. Even his fancy clothes, still finely pressed, looked dated and out of fashion. The newer and younger criminal fraternity was no longer interested in lorry hold ups or break ins. There were newer and easier ways of making money, and that was through the distribution of the very 'stuff' that had killed Girlie. It was a darker, meaner, and more dangerous underworld, where the likes of Bryan Mooney would not have survived. As I stated earlier, my uncle was an enigma. To him, crime was about more than the pursuit of money. I believe that there was something within him that needed the excitement, and the thrill.

I would return occasionally to London to see my family, and if he heard I was back he would usually pop in to say hello. He was not the cock sure man of my youth. To me, he had become a rather sad character. He never spoke of Girlie, but his swagger and spark were gone. His only topic of conversation was trains.

Apparently, he had joined a group that gave their spare time rebuilding old steam locomotives. The dapper fellow who was full of confidence was a memory, replaced by an old man whose conversation was limited to talking of his new pastime. It made me think of a word called retribution. Always keeping his emotion well hidden, l am confident that Bryan spent his last years shrouded by guilt.

Strangely, this character who had led much of his life as a criminal had always been proud of his roots. He remained proud to be the son of Denis Mooney, Liverpool magistrate, and ex Sergeant Major. For all his faults and transgressions, I always shared a bond with my uncle Bryan. He liked me from the first meeting in that tiny Garston kitchen in 1955. He always encouraged me musically. When we were alone, he would say that on his death I would be receiving this or getting that. I took it all with a pinch of salt. I just replied that any memorabilia to do with our family would be appreciated, but I wanted nothing of value. What I was trying to tell him was that I did not want anything that he acquired illegally. I knew he had a son somewhere, and if anything of value would prefer him to be the benefactor of his father's days of crime.

The last time I saw my uncle he was a man in his mid-eighties who was bedridden, and it was obvious that his time to depart was not far off. I did not go to his funeral.

I could not forgive him for his neglect of Girlie. I was also sure that the service would be attended by the sad old remnants of his criminal career, and I most certainly did not want to be a part of that. It therefore came as a surprise some time later to find out that I had been mentioned in his will, and that his executor wished to meet me at an address in Highbury.

Living in Jersey and having a young family it would take me a few weeks to organise, but eventually I found myself ringing the bell of a rather nice house at the rear of Highbury Square. A pleasant enough elderly lady opened the door and invited me in. She explained that she and her late husband had known Bryan for many years and that she was acting as his executor. I was amused later to find out that she and her husband had run a locksmith's shop in North London, ideal people to know when it came to picking locks or opening safes. Peeking into her lounge I recognised several pieces of beautiful furniture that had once graced Bryan's flat. Quite openly she spoke of my uncle with affection, and with a definite admiration for him. Though she never came out openly about their dealings, she did say that her late husband and my uncle had 'worked together' a lot in the past. As she was being slightly open with me, and as I thought there was nothing to lose, I asked her if my uncle enjoyed his way of life.

'He loved it son, he just loved the buzz.' She had

confirmed in those few words what I had always suspected.

Eventually she drew my attention to a large box. Inside were photo albums, documents, and various odd jewellery items. Uncle Bryan had done as I had asked of him and left anything relevant of our mutual family to me. Realising that others had been on the scene before me I did not ask questions, neither did I ask to see his will. He had left me what I had asked for and I was more than happy.

The family memorabilia were as valuable to me as Uncle Bryan's furniture was to her. It was a treasure trove of family history. It was also incredibly sad, for it included dozens of photos of Girlie and Helen. One photo stood out, and which I still find upsetting. It must have been taken in 1953 and shows a devoted and happy couple. A little baby girl is being proudly held by her mother. Alongside them stands the little girl's proud father, and in the background is a large car. It was a 1939 Black Jaguar!

THE FIGHTING BROTHERS, TRAGEDY, AND THE FAMILY BREAK UP.

The children of Denis and Margaret Sarah Mooney were six in number, five boys and one daughter. Leon had been the second born. Like my father, he too was enrolled at Liverpool Collegiate College and grew to be the athlete of the family, excelling in football, cricket, and of course American baseball. He fought in World War II and was wounded but recovered and was soon back in action.

Desmond like all his brothers was keen on sport as a lad. However, I do not think he was as involved as his older brother. He too fought in the war and was gravely injured in Italy and was eventually shipped home. His injuries were in the hip region and were such that he remained with a bad limp for the rest of his life. He remained at home till the death of his father in 1958. An Everton fanatic, he never missed a home match. I met him several times as a boy and he was a genuinely nice man. He met a nurse after his father's death and married. I believe they had three children, the first of which died as a baby, and was buried in the family grave.

Leslie was the youngest boy. I know nothing of him other than a naval photograph uncle Bryan gave me. He was a handsome young man, and he is pictured with a fellow sailor and two pretty girls. He had served as a submariner towards the end of the war. After being demobbed he went to Australia and joined the navy there, also serving on submarines. No one in the family heard from him again, until his death. We, and 1 presume others in our spread-out family, had been traced by Australian authorities. Leslie had passed away in his 80s in a naval home. He had obviously made a career out of the navy. He had never married and had left no will. He had a small amount of savings, so myself, my brothers, and other family members, received just over £1,000 each. I always felt it was a sad way to die. Leslie never wrote home after his departure for Australia, and it was about this time (1947), that the Mooney family started to split. I think 1 may have found the tragic reasons for this family break up.

PARTING OF THE WAYS

Margaret Mooney was 23 years old when she died. Three months later her mother Margaret Sarah joined her, dying from a broken heart. They both lie in Anfield Cemetery alongside Denis, husband, and father, in the grave that l found with Uncle Bryan in 1991.Neither my dad or Uncle Bryan had ever, or would ever, discuss the close deaths of their sister and mother. A lady l met in Skelmersdale that same year (1991) gave me information that would seem to explain the answer. She had replied to an ad l had placed in The Liverpool Echo asking if anyone recalled the Mooney family. Raised in the same Anfield Street, she had grown up alongside my dad's family. The information she gave me explains why the Mooney boys went their separate ways

During the war, apart from the bombing in the early years, Liverpool would have been an exciting place to be a teenage girl. Young British and foreign soldiers, sailors, and airmen frequented the town. Dance halls flourished, and being young, girls like Margaret would have lived for the moment. Up until the war she would probably have been restricted by a military minded father. The war changed those rules, and single women found a new freedom. According to my Skelmersdale lady, my young aunty caused a lot of worry to her parents that was to end in tragedy. At the end of the war, she got involved with a Chinese man and ran off with him. She would certainly not have had the approval of my grandfather in such a relationship, but being in her early twenties, she was free to do as she wished. I do not know if it was due to arguments at home, and it really does not matter, but Margaret left home without saying a word.

My grandfather had been a magistrate for many years and had many police friends. The word went out and they assured him they would find her. It was to take much longer than was hoped. A lengthy period would pass before word came that she was possibly in Chinatown.

Chinatown at that time had a reputation for being a part of Liverpool that lived by its own rules, so such news would have been horrendous. With Margaret's photograph in hand, both parents scoured the whole of Chinatown asking anyone who would listen if they had seen or heard anything of their only daughter. They eventually found her bedridden in a hovel. She was alone, and was ill with T.B. Chinatown back then was not a place where people willingly went, and had a reputation, legitimate or not, of opium usage. Even the police were hesitant to get involved in the area. They got her to hospital, then eventually, she returned to her home. That is all that l know, other than she died at her Anfield home aged 23, followed by a broken-hearted mother three months later. Though I have no confirmation, it is possible that her Chinese partner may have been a victim of a shameful episode that was carried out on the orders of the British government.

In 1946, 1,3000 Chinese sailors were rounded up and forcibly repatriated back to China. Special ships awaited them in the Mersey. They were picked up off the streets, from shops, and from their social clubs. Others had been tricked into reporting for outbound ships. None were given the chance to plead their case, and it was just forcible racial removal. Many were married, had children, and had lived and settled in Liverpool decades before. Those wives and mothers left behind were given no information on their men, leaving many oblivious and abandoned. Because they had married aliens, these poor women, many with children, would receive no support from the government and were on their own. As I explained, I have no idea if this was the reason for my auntie Margaret to be in such a poor condition, but the year was right, and with her ill health and general poor condition, it is a highly likely possibility.

I cannot conceive of how awful it must have been for Denis Mooney and his sons. I think it was these deaths that caused the breakup of the Mooney family. Each son had done their duty as their father wished. Each had survived warfare as their father had, but their mother and sister were dead, and it was those two that had bound them all together.

Bryan returned to his lucrative but very dubious life in London. Youngest son Leslie loved submarines, and applied, and was accepted as a submariner in the Australian Navy. He never returned and eventually ceased all contact with his father and brothers. Leon moved down south to Ongar near Epping Forest, started his own building business, married, and fathered four children. Apart from one brief brotherly get together (Leon, Bryan, and my dad) in the late fifties, Leon never kept in touch. My dad's life was with his young family on the other side of Liverpool, meaning that he would see his father very infrequently. We would go as a family, but I never felt any affinity with my grandfather. The only one who remained with his father was third eldest son Desmond. Partly due to his terrible wartime injury, Desmond remained under his father's roof until April 1958 when my grandfather died aged 77. He married late in life and moved outside Liverpool.

LONDON LIFE

1955-1966

So, there we were, three Liverpool kids, taken from everything we were accustomed to. Lost, but also realising that we now lived in one of the greatest and most historic places in the world. Brother Denis would feed our interest in London, as he always had with everything else. We found ourselves hungry for knowledge, wanting to find out as much about England's capital as we could.

Pemberton Gardens is in Archway, in the north London borough of Islington. It is a pleasant tree laden road that branches off the beginning of the A1 (the Great North Road) in Holloway. Though once a very residential road, by the mid-1950s the grand Victorian houses had lost their pre-war Luster. With massive housing shortages, most had been converted into unfurnished flats, their occupants occupying their own individual landings. My Uncle Bryan had leased three such houses in Pemberton Gardens from St John the Evangelist Church. Built in the 1830s, this grandiose Church of England structure still stands grandly at the road's southside entrance. A public transport depot had been erected in the street in 1907. In its time the sheds had been home to trams, but by the time we arrived in 1955, it was mainly a huge garage for trolleybuses.

A short time after our initial arrival Uncle Bryan moved us into a larger place further up the road. The move to London had been a traumatic time for everyone, but especially my mam. Amongst the many things she had to do was to get her boys placements in local schools for the start of the new term which was only weeks away. For Denis and John this didn't prove too difficult, but being born in 1946 I was more of a problem. Returning servicemen and the end of World War 11 had created a worldwide 'baby boom' leading to record classroom numbers. I can still recall being amused at one school where the headmistress declined my admission by telling my mam that the school was 'absolutely choc-a-bloc!' Everything eventually fitted into place, we found a school, but with my thick Garston accent there were difficult times ahead, both with teachers and with classmates. Both my parents had no difficulty finding work, and it didn't take my dad long to say goodbye to the menial jobs and be dressed in the suit his education warranted. As for us boys, well it was still the summer holidays, so we started checking out the vicinity. The one thing we knew was that we would never forget who we were. We had been taken from our roots for the best of reasons but were determined that at every given opportunity we would go back! In reality, however, we would have to conform and make the best of things, whilst never forgetting we were Liverpudlians, determined to retain our heritage.

Archway Underground Station lies at the bottom of Highgate Hill. This very steep hill, that on clear days offers stunning views of London, is said to be the place where Dick Whittington heard the bells of St. Mary-le-Bow telling him to turn around and try his luck once more in the city. According to the legend, he went on to become the Mayor of London four times. A dedication stone has stood on the hill since the 19th century and was complimented with the addition of a cat in 1964.

Highgate Village stands at the top of the hill and is like taking a trip back in time. We lads found it to be an intriguing place, and one we would constantly head for in the years that followed. Complete with its own village green, this Tudor style village of shops pubs and beautiful houses was a well-known drinking place for Charles Dickens who resided there for a short period in 1832.Both his parents, his daughter and his wife Catherine were buried in Highgate Cemetery. That cemetery was another fascinating place of history, proving that wealth cannot stop the inevitable. The cemetery is divided into two sections, east and west. Between them they have given occupancy to over 170,000 residents, one of whom is the father of communism Karl Marx. Mr Marx lies in the newer section, and his grave, which he probably would have objected to as being decadent, attracts tens of thousands of homages making believers each year. I have one memory of being nearby his resting place in the late 1950s and a coach pulling up to the gates. One by one some of the most dismally dressed men and women emerged and made their way timidly to the grave. I had thought at the time that they must be trusted Russian Party members, but in reality, they could have come from anywhere in the Eastern bloc. They all looked old before their time and their movements were well scrutinised by their obvious' party minders!'

The other and much older cemetery could only have been described as macabre. Looking down over the city, the position of the burial ground would have been seen as the ideal resting place for London's wealthy and elite. Wanting to keep alive a show of their lifetime assets, they had ensured their final resting places were vaults and tombs that were opulent, lavish, and grand, with several built in Italian marble. That opulence was how the cemetery remained into the new century. Two world wars, and lack of funds, led the council to concentrate on more important issues, and the old part of the cemetery fell into terrible disrepair. Pathways were left to become overgrown. The windows of the vaults had been smashed by vandals. Trees, bushes, and ivy were left to gruesomely grow and cover hundreds of graves. The whole area had become like a scene from a Dracula movie. Hardly surprising then that the Hammer film company used the cemetery in many of their 1960s successful horror films. Creepy as it was, it was still open to the public, and not unnaturally was of great interest to three inquisitive Garston lads. We knew there was tremendous history under our feet, much of which was explained on the headstones. Less ornate than the tombs and vaults, but still the work of true craftsmen, were the graves of poets, writers, and artists. During the 1970s the authorities wanted to bulldoze the area, but luckily local enthusiasts purchased it for a nominal sum. Today it is looked after by local volunteers and many parts have been returned to their former glory. It is now a tourist option and attracts visitors from all over the world.

During the industrial revolution, Highgate Village, with its proximity to the city became an ideal place for the wealthy to reside. Indeed, properties are still much sought after, especially by the celebrities of today. Amongst those who have chosen to reside in the village at one time or another have been Ringo Starr, Lulu, Jude Law, Kate Moss, Liam Gallagher, Jimi Hendrix, Annie Lennox, and Jamie Oliver. Indeed, such is the relaxed aura of the village that it is not unusual to see some well-known faces having a meal or a pint in the local hostelries. One famous lady we often saw with her shopping basket was Margaret Rutherford, famous at the time for her appearances as the eccentric upper-class lady in countless British films who would go on to be internationally famous for her interpretation of Agatha Christie's Miss Marples.

During the remaining days we had before joining our new schools, and with both parents working, we kept going back to the same area that looked down across the beautiful vista of London. We discovered that Highgate was adjacent to Hampstead Heath, a 790-acre area of greenery, woods, and ponds. This was what we wanted. This was as near to the Garston and Speke shore as we could get. This was where we would return as often as possible, just for the joy of nature. Looking back, we were three very fit lads who walked for miles, just as we had done along the Mersey.

Having learnt to swim in Garston Baths, the pastime

had become a very important part of our lives. So naturally when we heard that there were swimming ponds adjacent to the heath, and never having swum in fresh water, we set off with our towels and 'cozzies.' Parliament Hill Fields has several large fishing ponds renowned for their abundance of carp, bream, pike and roach. Two of them allow separate sex swimming. We didn't realise what that was until we entered the "men only' open air large wooden shed. It was a beautiful sunny August day, and we were confronted by dozens of mainly elderly naked men! I was not yet nine years old and can remember being shocked to the core. All were bronzed, and all seemed totally oblivious to those around them. I had heard of naturists, and looking back I guess that's what they were. I certainly learned that no two men are alike in one department of their physical assets! Certainly, none of them seemed to be there for the swimming! Homosexuality was still illegal, so I suppose a few were there for other reasons! Well, I wasn't about to ask, within seconds I was in the coldest but most exhilarating water I had ever swum in. For the next few years, even in the coldest of weather, the Mooney boys had enjoyment from something that cost them nothing. There was also a council owned public swimming baths not too far away, one of the many that

London once had, but which are all sadly gone. In those early years in London, we utilized what was known as The London Transport Red Rover ticket. For a minimum cost children could use all trolly and Routemaster buses and travel anywhere in central London. It allowed us such great opportunities to see the whole of the city. We brothers got to know the city like the back of our hands. Even today, I would never get lost in London.

I told earlier of our love of cinema. Well, there were no shortages of silver screens in North London, and at one time or another, we went inside all of them! At one end of our street stood the newly opened Rank owned Odeon, and at the other, the much older and smaller A.B.C. cinema The Empire. Both were frequented by us every week, as well as The Palace, a flea pit near Archway Station. There were also three other cinemas within walking distance, so we boys were spoilt for choice. The 1950s to me was the period that Hollywood and British studios were at their best. Long queues for the cinema were still a regular occurrence handled by grandly dressed doormen, whilst inside the ice cream lady still stood in front of the silver screen during the intermission. During that fabulous period of change, we were introduced to 3D, Cinemascope, Stereophonic

Sound, Cinerama, Panavision, Technorama, and Todd AO. To a young kid it was magical, showing the wonders of America in such glorious colours and scenic splendour. Come to think of it, back then, everything a young lad like me dreamed about came out of the U.S.A. The movies, the music, and the clothes. In the years that followed, my birthday treat was to be taken to a West End cinema. They were always grander venues. I saw Ben Hur for my 12th birthday in Leicester Square, and South Pacific at The Dominion, Tottenham Court Road for my 13th.

My early school days in London seemed to revolve around a lot of fighting. I would have spoken in one of the most guttural accents ever to come out of Liverpool, with native Garston brogue being particularly sharp. The term 'taking the mickey' was one I was not familiar with in Liverpool, but I soon learned what it meant in London. I was the brunt of one particular kid in my class who took delight in poking fun at the way I spoke until I snapped and taught him a lesson in the gentle art of receiving a good whack on the gob. Whilst he never bothered me again, there were older and bigger kids who did. I learned over time to refine my words, without ever losing my scouse accent. I did my best to slot in, but my home city and the Garston shore was never far from my thoughts.

It was still the age of the steam train, and London stations gave young lads like us a wonderful opportunity to witness the last days of some of the most beautiful steam powered engines in the world. The main stations like Euston, Paddington, Victoria, and Kings Cross, had been run by private companies prior to privatisation, so each had their own styled engines. Today they would have called boys like us anoraks, but we just loved steam trains and felt lucky to still be able to see such regal locomotives in all their glory. We had The Observers Book of British Steam Trains, and those we were able to tick off were The Mallard, The Flying Scotsman, The Brighton Belle, The Blue Peter, and The Brittania, all for the price of a one penny platform ticket. Much of those early years in London are now a blur, but I do recall our Sundays. As in Liverpool, our parents would always take their boys out. We would go to all the wonderful museums and parks, as well the places of history like The Tower of London, St Pauls Cathedral and Buckingham Palace. My dad was also very partial to Speakers Corners at the Marble Arch entrance to Hyde Park where individuals could stand on a rostrum and virtually say anything they liked without fear of arrest.

Aunty Maggie became a regular visitor. For a lady who had not ventured far from Merseyside she adapted well to travelling to London by train. Always one to go out downtown on Fridays, she kept up her weekly habit by journeying to the Strand where she knew of a Yates's Wine Lodge. I can remember us three boys taking her to the pictures to see the classic Ealing comedy The Ladykillers. The main character was a little old lady who is duped into renting out a room for a motley bunch of thieves planning a robbery at nearby Kings Cross Station. Possibly because of the little old lady, Aunty Maggy loved it. She seemed to get great joy from the cinema but would never have dreamed of going on her own. Another film we took her to was Seven Brides for Seven Brothers a musical.

My dad had always liked a flutter and began to frequent the dog track at Haringey. Whilst there he saw a sign advertising a future event. The Moscow State Circus was world renowned, and whilst I look back in shame, I was part of a generation that didn't appreciate the animal cruelty that took place behind the scenes of such travelling shows. I laughed along with all the other kids at the sight of brown bears riding converted motorcycles with no concern for the poor creatures.

Variety shows were still going in theatres outside of

the West End and North London still had two such venues. The Finsbury Park Empire was not too far, and we would often go to see variety shows in their final death throes. We brothers would get the cheapest seats up in the Gods, and if we could afford it would rent the sixpenny binoculars that were attached to the seats. With the arrival of rock n roll in the States many American singers were coming to England for work. We also used to go to Collins Music Hall, next to Islington Green in The Angel, Islington. This really was old time in the real sense, with a bar at the rear. It had operated since 1863 and closed its doors in 1958 due to a fire. Once ITV came on the scene in the autumn of 1955, such venues were on borrowed time anyway. I am pleased that we frequented such places, as the kids at my school seemed to go nowhere or know very little of the city of their birth.

Petticoat Lane Market was a regular destination for the family on Sunday mornings. Strewn through bombed out streets, the market was truly a bastion of a London that is sadly gone. Predominantly made up of East End Jews, the language was like poetry to the ears. Those were the real old cockneys, natural comedians with so much cynical, but harmless humour. Our favourites were the guys selling crockery. They seemed to be able to balance and swing their products so expertly. On Saturday afternoons, a short bus ride took us to The Angel Market, but it was much smaller and lacking the atmosphere of Petticoat Lane.

The England of the mid-fifties was still a country at odds with itself. Up until 1958 it still had National Service, and to some degree it still held international respect for its armed services. For the man in the street however it could still be a bleak place to live and work. Being young meant conformity and falling in line with previously held attitudes. Then out if the blue a 30-year-old stocky American who adorned himself with a kiss curl introduced rock n roll to the British public. Glenn Ford was the star in the M.G.M. movie 'Blackboard Jungle. 'The opening titles showed a new inexperienced teacher (Ford) arriving at a New York school renowned for its hoodlums. As soon as the shot opens. Wham! Haley begins his song; one o'clock, two o'clock, three o'clock, rock! From that moment on, Britain changed. Rock 'n' roll had arrived, and the world of popular music had changed from clean cut crooners to grease haired rockers. Rock was snapped up by a new emerging population of youngsters who had made it their own. Rock symbolised rebellion, and defiance against conformity. Requiring a face of youth and good looks, a kid from Mississippi named Elvis Presley fitted the bill, and it wasn't long before Bill Haley was relegated to history. There were no British commercial radio stations back then, so the listening to the new music was limited to struggling to get a decent signal from Radio Luxembourg or putting up with what the BBC Light Programme deemed as suitable. BBC T.V. was a bit more daring (probably due to concerns about the new ITV channel) and put out a Saturday night pop show called The Six 5 Special. It was very British and very Aunty BBC in its delivery, but it was better than nothing. The proper presentation of what young people wanted would be several more years down the road when ITV showed how rock n roll should be delivered. Producer Jack Good realised that the kids wanted no chat from aging comperes, and that the whole focus of the show must be aimed at the young. Oh Boy just went straight into it with the likes of Cliff Richard, Marty Wilde, and Billy Fury going from one number straight into the next. Occasionally, top American artists like Conway Twitty and Brenda Lee were featured. It was followed later by a sequel show called 'Boy meets Girls,' which utilized bigger American artist like Johnny Cash.

There had been another kind of music that captured British captured kids' imaginations, and it was known as skiffle! We did not know it at the time of our move, but the previous occupants had been a Mr Anthony Donegan and his wife. Lonnie Donegan would soon be known as the King of Skiffle, and it was his popularity and use of guitar that saw thousands of British lads buying guitars. The sale of the guitars increased in the U.K. from 5,000 to nearly 200,000 in one year. Amongst that multitude of 'wannabe skifflers were three of the Beatles, Eric Clapton, Hank Marvin, Joe Brown, Albert Lee, and most of the guitar playing musicians that put 1960s British pop on the global map. Tony Donegan, like so many other musicians moved in the same musical circles as Uncle Bryan and the two had become friends. Skiffle was a very American form of improvised music that was a mixture of black blues, hillbilly, folk, bluegrass, and gospel, all thrown in, and played easily on guitar with the normal use of just three chords.it was also played with non-musical instruments like washboards for percussion, and tea chests, which with the aid of a broom handle, and a long piece of strong string, was transferred into a double bass. Donegan's first solo record (he had recorded previously in the Chris Barber Jazz Band playing banjo) was a song by black blues artist Huddie Leadbetter. Rock Island Line was so different from what normally came out of

British recording studios that it became a huge hit, and even reached No 8 on the American charts, a feat no other British artist had ever achieved. It even caught the attention of Ed Sullivan, who was host to America's top T.V. show. CBS flew Donegan to New York and put him on Sullivan's Saturday Night Variety Show, beating The Beatles by several years! Rock Island Line went on to sell 3 million copies. It must be remembered that in those bleak post war British days that all things American were a beacon of light to British kids. Those skiffle songs told tales with a poetic imagery of train crashes, the building of great dams, card sharks, saloon shootings, prisons and the hard grind of picking cotton. All subjects that conjured up romantic pictures of America in the minds of British kids. I had my German guitar and found skiffle easy to play. I was studying my chords and trying to emulate whatever I could. I had a good ear, and after much pain, the blisters on the end of my fingers had hardened. I was discovering how to play jingles from the T.V. and many of the little rifts from records. No one ever complained at my efforts, as by that time Denis was working and had bought a radiogram. I can put my hand on my heart and say that neither of our parents ever once complained about me clanking on the guitar or Denis incessantly playing his records. Ours was a very musical abode. Always encouraging, my mam would treat me with new guitar strings that she brought back from the music shops in Charing Cross Road. Sadly, 1 knew no one in London, apart from my uncle Bryan who tinkered with guitars, so it became a single-handed hobby. That's how it continued for several years, just me, and my hard to play German guitar. Oddly enough, few of my school friends knew of my guitar playing. It was just something I kept to myself.

School days came and went, and to be honest were not the best years of my life. I was certainly not academic, but neither was I thick. The teachers were of a very poor standard except for those who taught English. I seemed to have a gift when it came to written composition and was often praised for my stories and poems. Our English teacher for the first two years was a man called Edward Blishen. He had written two quite successful novels, both of which were semi-autobiographical regarding a teacher in a post war overcrowded north London school. He was also a regular on the radio as a storyteller on BBC Children's Hour. To get small praise from him is still something I take as a wonderful compliment. I had eventually made friends, but none that were much more than good acquaintances. I always felt different, with my accent of course, but in my general outlook and interests, especially when it came to music. Most of the lads I knew would be listening to Elvis, Cliff Richard or whoever was in vogue. I liked my rock to be a little less commercial and rawer, and listened to American artists like Chuck Berry, Little Richard, and Fats Domino. I liked Buddy Holly very much because I knew he wrote his own material and was different from the norm. However, because of my Garston education into music from those thin walls, I was still a massive fan of country music, especially Hank Williams, Hank Snow, and the new boy on the scene, Johnny Cash. Country music was seen as hick music in London, and probably still is. I think it's their loss, not mine.

During those mid to late 1950s years, I had returned on many occasions to Liverpool. I would normally go with my mam on the overnight Crossville coach from Victoria Coach Station and stay downtown at my Aunty Joan's. During the day I would go to Garston. There was always some kid or other to hang out with. Obviously, those I had known and spent my early years with had changed, as I suppose I had. There wasn't the welcome mat I had envisioned, but I was happy just being under the bridge. Prior to our leaving for an Easter trip to

Liverpool in 1957, my dad had asked that we visit my grandfather in Anfield. I was about as enthusiastic about going to see him as my mam was, but she promised she would. My mam did not like my grandad. He had always been snooty towards her and had made her feel as though he was looking down on her. The daughter of a window cleaner, my mam's background was very different to my dad's. I had never felt comfortable in his presence. I think we boys were in awe of him and realised he was a well-respected man within the city, but he was never warm towards us. We would perhaps go three times a year, always dressed in our best bib and tucker, but he never came to us in Garston, and I do not recall any obvious signs of affection when we went to Anfield. Perhaps it was his ex-army and military background that made him feel the need to act superior?

Prior to going to Anfield, we had spent the morning in Woolton, visiting an elderly Jewish doctor's widow my mam had cleaned for. I can still hear the chimes of the beautiful grandfather clock that stood in the hall, and picture the colourful, well- tended garden. I had been to the house on one prior occasion some years before when I was probably about seven years old. I had endured terrible earache all night, and my mam had decided to keep me off school. She had taken me with her to work and I can remember her buying me a little drawing book to keep me occupied. I had sat at a large table in the ornate kitchen merrily doodling while she did her chores. The elderly lady had been very sympathetic and had even given me a glass of tizer to drink.

Anfield is a long way from Woolton, so our arrival wasn't until about 1.30 that afternoon. Finchley Road is just a short walk down from Priory Road and consists of just 24 houses. I had pulled a few faces as we got off the bus, muttering under my breath. I didn't like going to see my grandad as I never felt comfortable. It was as though he was still a Sgt Major, and we were his underlings being inspected. I have no memory of him ever sitting down. Had he not been a soldier, his posture would have been that of an upright police sergeant questioning a suspect.

My mam knocked tentatively at first on the door of number 12. No reply. Her knock became louder, but still no reply. Feeling relieved, I told her that we should go. She held my hand, said something about having promised my dad and walked me around to the back entry. The back yard door was unlocked, so we walked through and once again my mam began knocking.

Eventually I convinced her that we should go. We had barely got halfway through the yard door when, still in his pyjamas, Denis Mooney, the ex-Sergeant Major and Justice of the Peace, opened his bedroom window and popped his head out. "Who is it?" he asked in a tone that was anything but happy. "It's Vi, and I promised Denis that I would take his youngest son to see his grandfather, well here he is, I've done as I was asked." With that she tugged on my arm, we walked through the entry, back up to Priory Road, and caught the bus to town. I never saw him again. He died in the Spring of the next year. After a life of adventure and duty, old age had made his life empty, and he had taken to his bed. My uncle Desmond, who worked as a telephonist for the Post Office still lived with his father, due to having been badly injured during the war. It was him that found his dead father in bed. His death certificate said that he had died from pneumonia, he was 79. Printed in The Liverpool Echo, Desmond wrote a wonderful obituary for the father he had never left. Neither I or my mother or brothers attended his funeral in Anfield Cemetery but learned that it had been a very military ceremony with regulars of The Kings Regiment (Liverpool) old comrades, and representatives of the Liverpool Police and members of the Judiciary. It was what he would have wanted, and though a virtual stranger to me I am very proud of him, for he was a very driven and honourable Liverpudlian man of his time.

I was 13, it was Easter, and I was in Liverpool with my mam once more. As I always did, I was checking through the cinema lists of the Echo. Nearly one whole page was devoted to the cinemas that remained in the city. I noticed a larger ad for a rock 'n' roll show that was on at The Liverpool Empire. Two American boys Eddie Cochran (Summertime Blues, C'mon Everybody, Something Else) and Gene Vincent (Be Bob A-Lula, Lotta Lovin) were topping the bill, along with Liverpool's very own Billy Fury, and the cockney guitar wizard Joe Brown. I pleaded with my mam to take me after I found out that they were doing cheaper matinee shows. It was hardly the kind of show most 50-year-old women would normally attend, but she loved it. I was to read some years later that John, Paul and George had also attended the shows, though I think they did so separately. This was rock 'n' roll as it was meant to be, not sanitised, just the real McCoy. Even Billy Fury, who initially copied Elvis was special, as most of the songs he sang were ones he had penned himself. As for Joe Brown, well he was probably Britain's best rock n roll guitarist of the time. It came as a shock one week later when my mam appeared with a newspaper informing me that Cochran was dead, killed in a car accident. I have seen many artists 'live' on stage, but that show was very, very special, especially that young American boy Eddie Cochran.

It was during that Easter of 1960 that I had got reacquainted with Tommy who, along with his brother Neil I had gone to Banks Road School with. Tommy had always been very friendly with my eldest brother Denis, but in fact all the brothers on both sides seemed to have to have been pally with each other. The shore had a lot to do with that friendship, for if we were there, they were there. On my trips back to Garston Tommy and I began to share a special bond. That mutual interest was music. Our tastes were very much the same, both of us having a fondness for Country and American rock n roll. He was older than me, and I guess he took me under his wing. I found myself no longer staying downtown at Aunty Joan's but staying in Garston at Tommy's. Looking back, it probably sounds funny, but we slept three in a bed, Neil on the left, me in the middle, and Tommy on the right. We thought nothing of it, that's just the way things were, you made do! Neither of Tommy's parents objected, and I soon felt like one of the family. I started taking my guitar with me as Tommy had bought one and was keen to learn. Sadly, he was never able to progress far, but he had the ability to play the simple chords that were required for Country. We would sit in his kitchen doing our best to bang out some numbers, and as with my parents in London, nobody ever objected. So, my trips to Liverpool began to take on a musical aspect, and for the first time I had someone to play guitar and sing with. On one trip it was decided that we would show off our skills, such as they were, in some of the under the bridge pubs. By that time, I was fifteen and had left school. Strangely I was never questioned as to my age, so Tommy educated me into alcohol. Black and Tans, Black Velvets, Stout, Mild, I tried them all at one time and learned which ones to avoid through trial and error, leaving my mark in many gent's toilets. One such pub was The Victoria on the corner of Sinclair Street and King Street. It was a dockers pub as basic as they come with wooden floorboards. A barroom full of big burly dockers was as good as anywhere to show off my new guitar. Some months earlier my mam had won the big prize at the bingo and shared her winnings with her sons. It was an opportunity to get myself a 12-string guitar. I felt so proud going to London's West End and entering Selmers in Charing Cross Road and having the money to get a decent guitar. The sound of a 12 string is one I have always liked since hearing the black blues player, Huddie Leadbetter. They are much louder and have double strings, one of which is an octave higher that gave the instrument an almost mandolin sound. As with everything in life, nothing is perfect, and the 12 strings must be tuned to 100% accuracy. Someone recently commented that unlike some guitar players, my guitar was always perfectly tuned. If I had one talent, it was that I had a very good musical ear that stayed with me through the years when it became essential to be in perfect tune. Well by the time I got my 12-stringer tuned to my satisfaction in the Vic the dockers were getting restless. We got there eventually and though there was no rapturous response we both enjoyed ourselves that night and had no complaints from anyone. From that time on, where I went, that guitar went. Soon after that time I started working. That meant that instead of the long journey by coach to Liverpool, I was able to take the overnight train from Euston. The train coaches back then were far more intimate with passengers sitting opposite each other in enclosed compartments. It happened quite a few times that some scouser would ask me to play my guitar during the journey, and sometimes an impromptu sing-along took place. It really was a very different world, and one I was so glad to have been part of.

I haven't mentioned girls, and yes of course in my early teenage years there were girls. I was as interested in girls as any other lad, and there were no real shortage, but always felt awkward, and uncomfortable with them, never knowing how to behave, or what things to say. So their faces are long gone from my memory. There is however one girl friend from when I was 15 who through the wonders of Facebook found me 55 years later. Sadly Josie had been widowed for several years having nursed her husband through terminal cancer, but we keep in touch with a long distance friendship and see each other several times a year.

There was one special relationship I had when I was 17. It was with a lovely lady who was much older than me. It was an impossible situation, and one carried out in great secrecy. Out of respect for her memory I will merely say that she was a very important part of my journey from adolescence to manhood, and I have no regrets.

I never went to The Cavern as a teenager. When I went to Garston, I normally spent the whole time under the bridge. As l said, Tommy was older than me, so we would more so frequent the local places like The Woodcutters, or The Blue Union. Tommy was courting a girl from Speke by this time, and I guess I was becoming a bit of a wallflower, but we still talked music and strummed our guitars. Luckily for me, Neil had come back from a stint in the merchant navy, was nearer to my age, and I attached myself to him.

This would have been during the beginnings of the Mersey Beat Explosion. Being more of an American rock n roll lad, I hadn't paid too much attention to four lads from south Liverpool who had got into the charts with 'Love me do.' Of course, I had heard the song and liked it, but it didn't capture my interest. Then I saw them on T.V. I liked their style of clothing, I liked their humour, and gradually over the months I became a huge Beatles follower. They were so full of life, and fun. No one at that time had seen anything like the hysteria of the teenage girls from all over the country. Consequently, every lad wanted to be a look-alike Beatle. Previously, lads had pushed their hair back to look like Elvis. Suddenly there was a cultural revolution, and the 'Elvis look' was out! Brycream sales must have plummeted! Greased back hair was suddenly pushed forward, and looking back there were many men that looked quite ridiculous. Winklepicker shoes came on the scene also, so sales of corn plasters increased. It was great for me. The Liverpool accent I had tried not to lose had suddenly become trendy and cool. Every newspaper was headlining about the Merseybeat sound and Beatlemania. I truly believe that there will never be a period like the 1960s. After conquering Europe, The Beatles conquered America. Their style of dress evolved, and so did that of the ordinary man in the street. London became the fashion capital of the world. Mini skirts, tights and hot pants, not just for the teenager, but for the older woman. For me, being from Liverpool and being young made me stand out. In 1963 and 1964, The Beatles had a special Christmas Show at The Finsbury Park Astoria. Some of my mates were going, so l decided that I would pay my 15 shillings and go and see for myself just how good a band they were. The compere was a man later disgraced for his sexual preferences of young girls. Strange how things turned out for the 3-legged Jeg the Peg man Rolf Harris! All the artists on the show (apart from Harris) were managed by Brian Epstein, Liverpool's very own impresario. I remember seeing The Fourmost, Billy J. Kramer, and Cilla Black before the whole building erupted with screams. I have honestly never witnessed such hysteria with girls crying and fainting. Due to the volume of the female screams I never heard a thing from those four boys from Liverpool, but I realised that I was witnessing history. I knew that these lads were not just a flash in the pan, but were something very, very special. Their first album reiterated that for me. Though there were many cover versions as well as Lennon and McCartney songs, the whole album was recorded in one day, was almost perfect, and showed just how good they were, not only in their harmonies, but in their musicianship. Even my parents, always young at heart, bought tickets to see and experience Beatlemania. I find that fact a wonderful insight into just who they were as people. I felt very proud of them. The Beatles created a musical storm that would gather in momentum and would go on to change the world.

I have always felt that the 'baby boomers' were the lucky generation. We were born into a bankrupt struggling country, but slowly and gradually we saw things improving. We endured in very poor housing when we were tots, but we knew no difference. I think the streets toughened us up. Being outside and always up to some mischief was all good experience for later life. Besides, we never went hungry, and though treats were rare, we probably ate healthier food than today's children. We dressed in the basic street apparel with patches in our pants, but we were always well dressed if we went anywhere.

As I said regarding Neil, he was nearer my age, and we have looked out for each other all our lives. He had a had a bunch of mates, some of whom had cars, and they liked to get out of Garston. I was 18 and looking for fun. We would drive outside the city and visit live music dances halls around Runcorn and Frogham. Everywhere was 'live' music with some great groups, wherever you went in the Liverpool areas.

The subject of Jersey kept creeping into the conversation with Neil and some of his mates. There was talk of them going back to do another season. I was to learn that Jersey was a great place for the young during the summer months, and there was lots of seasonal work. I didn't even know where Jersey was on the map. I knew it was an island, and it was a name l was very familiar with as my mam had often said how much she would love to go there. Not only that, but my uncle Cyril would tell me he had worked a few seasons in Jersey just after the war at one of its most popular hotels and had loved it. So, the first seeds regarding Jersey were placed in my mind years before.

I left school aged fifteen, and l had no regrets. During the last two years spent there I had learned little, somehow, I had retained my interest in composition. English teachers were always complimentary about my imagination, but there was always a limit to their interest. The powers that be decided to change my Secondary Modern Boys School into a huge Mixed Comprehensive, one of the first in London. We were the guinea pigs in the capital's new educational experiment. Classrooms were scattered all over the Archway area, even in disused chapels. Once you had finished one class you would walk half a mile to the next. I could not wait to leave but had no idea what to do with my life. I had been offered and accepted an electrician's apprenticeship, only because other boys had done so. I began work at a small company about a 40-minute walk from home. I started in the January of 1962, and due to early morning rain, remained soaked throughout my first day. It was at the end of that day I found out that I had to pay all my own bus and tube fare and be at the job sight for 8 o'clock regardless of where the job was. Some of our work was several bus changes, and I soon realised the job would be costing me money I didn't have! I lasted two weeks! There was no shortage of work, so for the next several years I drifted aimlessly from one job to another. My brother John had got himself into work he grew to love as a steel erector. It involved a lot of going up and down the country to where the next big job was. He met Rita in Bridlington, and they have a successful marriage that has lasted for over half a century. Denis sadly never married but spent his days reading and betting on his beloved horses. He would have made a great historian. He now resides in a care home, having returned to the city of his birth. He did so after the death of our mother, whom he stayed with until she passed on.

Over the winter of 1965 I realised that my life was going nowhere; I had to get out of London. Liverpool would have been my preferential choice, but the unemployment was horrendous, although my brother John had gone back and found work on the tugs. I thought of warmer climates. I dreamed of some sun and adventure, and from what I had heard, Jersey seemed to be the right place for both. I decided that I would work hard and save as much as I could during the winter months and fly to Jersey the following Spring. I was lucky in the fact that I had a nighttime job with lots of overtime. Mac Fisheries was a Unilever Company, and its main depot was at Finsbury Park. At its peak, the company had 400 shops, but by the time I started working there in 1964, that number had reduced to 50. Those remaining shops were spread out across the southern regions of England in the High streets of affluent areas. The company sold fish, fruit and vegetables all top quality, as well as a few dairy products. Alongside the depot was a railway that brought ice packed fresh fish swiftly from eastern seaports like Lowerstoft. Scottish salmon also arrived in top condition from Scotland, and Dutch freshwater fish came in via Rotterdam. My hours were officially 11:00 p.m. until 7 a.m. but if your work was finished you were allowed to leave and go home to your nice warm bed. Once a week after work, several of us used to catch the early morning bus to Smithfield Meat Market where the pubs were open till 9 in the morning. We were given a weekly fish ration from Mac Fisheries and would exchange our plaice or cod package with an equal weight in pork chops from the market porters.

I had intended to go on my own to Jersey in April of 1966, thinking I could probably meet up with some Garston lads. One of the London fellas I hung out with said he was interested in joining me, so we both spent the winter saving up our money. I wasn't too sure how it would work out, but at least it meant I wasn't going to be jetting off to a strange place on my own. He was a very stable lad, had good parents, and I knew he had a head on his shoulders. His name was Eric, and he wanted to join the fire service later that year, so he wanted a bit of freedom before doing so. It was only going to be for less than six months anyway, so there was plenty of time to enjoy being young.

My mother told me that she had a difficult time when I was born. She had slipped into a coma and saw her brother (he had recently died of tuberculosis) Alfie standing in front of a huge glow of light. She said he was calling for her to join him. Thankfully the midwife gave her a slap and she rejoined the living. I tell this story because being the youngest, my brother John would accuse me of being our mam's "blue eyed boy." I suppose it was true, but maybe the difficulty of my birth had something to do with it. I wasn't outwardly aware but looking back I suppose she did keep a special eye out for me. I don't think she did so consciously, but when you are a kid you grab whatever attention you are given. I also mention this because I knew she would find my leaving home difficult. I know she did, but she never tried to stand in my way. I guess she knew that once I had spread my wings that she had lost her 'blue eyed boy' forever.

FLIGHT TO THE SUN

April 1966

The flight to Jersey was very different from the hassle one gets today. You simply went to Victoria Station and did all your checking in at a special shop that British United had at the platform's entry point. We never saw our luggage till we arrived in Jersey. I had flown before when I went to Spain's Costa Brava the previous summer with another friend Finton, a Dublin lad I had met at school. Gazing out the plane window, the sun was shining as we took our first glimpse of Jersey. We saw the cliffs and then cruised over one beautiful long stretch of sand that we learned later was St Oeuns Bay. Something within me told me that this was the beginning of a new chapter in my life, and that this island was another step up the ladder for me.

We had worked out a plan of what we would do on arrival. We knew that St Helier was the only town on the island, so we would get a taxi and ask the drivers advice on recommending a guest house away from the town centre. Having booked into our very basic but clean accommodation for a week, it was early afternoon by the time we had unpacked. Our first Jersey abode was situated in Val Plaisant, a long road that led straight into the heart of St Helier. We had time to do things and wanted to check in to the Social Centre and fill in whatever paperwork was involved. What we really wanted to do was to get all the sensible things out the way and learn the rest as we went along. I can't remember much about that first week other than we did a lot of walking, interspersed with a liberal amount of drinking and eating. I expect we were curious about the island, and took several bus journeys to various tourist spots, used the beaches, and did a lot of walking. We had also managed to find ourselves digs. We had soon learned that the chances of a flat were almost zero. 'Sleeping only' was a term we became very familiar with. Flats in Jersey were probably out of our financial ability to afford anyway, so we moved into the bedroom of a family home. Our new digs had two single beds and a cupboard for hanging our clothes. It was on the east of town, a thirty-minute walk from the St Helier bus terminus. The owners seemed like a nice friendly young couple, and anyway, we would be more out than in. We were told the rules and regulations, and as it was only for the coming summer, we agreed that it would suit our purpose.

Known as the Weighbridge area, the bus station seemed to be the main hub of town. We were young, and if we had to rough it, we knew we could cope. Being with someone for 24 hours a day can be irksome, but we got on quite well initially, probably because we had no choice but to do everything together. Eric had the gift of the gab when it came to girls, so we did what 19-year-old boys who are away from home are supposed to do.

THE HONOUR OF SERVING

The Jersey system of government was, and is, totally different to that in Great Britain. The island (which is only 6 miles by 9 miles) had been given the right of self-government by Charles II because of its loyalty to the Royalist cause during the Cromwellian Civil War. Its allegiance therefore is to the British monarchy, and not to the English Government. In 1966 we were surprised to learn that capital punishment was still the law, even though murderers had for several years seen their sentences commuted to life in prison. The use of the 'cat of the nine tails' was also lawful, but it too had ceased in the early 1960's. Within the law, and plain to see by the names of the streets and roads, there was still a very Norman influence. Only 18 miles from Normandy, Jersey had been heavily influenced by its Norman neighbours with its laws and its customs, but the locals are fiercely loyal to the British Crown. Because of its self-governing ability it has low tax rates and is described by those opposed to such places as an offshore tax haven.

Known locally as The Honorary System, in the 1960s when I arrived, the parliamentary members were unpaid, and ran the island because they felt it was their honour to do so. That system dated back hundreds of years, possibly back to Norman times. There was, and still is a professional paid police force, but there is also an honorary police force, made up of members of the public. At that time the latter had no uniforms or any clothing to prove who they were, and there was an obvious undercurrent of friction between the two. Both forces supposedly worked in unison, but there was ill feeling. One anachronism was that only the top policeman of the parishes (known as the Centeniers) had the power of arrest.

The Jersey members of Parliament are Senators, who have an island-wide mandate, Deputies who are voted in by the residents of the parish they represent, and the twelve Constables (Connetables), who are the head figures in each of the twelve parishes. The sittings of the members are overseen and adjudicated by the Bailiff, who is the monarch's representative. When I went to Jersey such practices seemed archaic, but I gradually found myself in admiration of men who would carry out such unpaid duties just for the honour of serving their island.

Much has changed in the years since my arrival. Politicians are now paid and the honorary police have relinquished many of their powers

LIFE ON THE FARM

Unfortunately the job scenario was proving more difficult than we had anticipated. We had been able to get odd days down at the dock as casual one day dockers. I learned how degrading it is to stand in a line and have a tally man walk past or pick you out for a day's work. On the few days we did this, the docks were particularly busy, so we were lucky, and it was cash in hand at the end of the day. We also got a job in a coal merchants, but although we didn't object to hard work, carrying huge bags of coal across farmyards and up steps was not to our taste. We learned that to get a job, the best way was to get early copies of the local newspaper The Jersey Evening Post. Each weekday afternoon, people would queue outside the premises of the paper hoping to get one of the first copies as soon as they had come off the presses. A man would appear at the front entrance with the first copies in bundles which he would unfold and then duly collect your cash. We devised a plan that if Eric got into a nearby phone booth and pretended to be talking, I could get a copy as quickly as possible then run to the phone box. Once inside we could scrutinise the jobs columns and make phone calls. One particular ad caught our eye, it was for nurserymen. The idea of being in the sun under glass growing tomatoes appealed to two city lads. We tried the number but to no avail. The name of the nursery was printed and there were several cabs parked nearby. We both seemed to think as one. St John is Jersey's most northerly parish (there are 12 parishes). In 1966, there were still dozens of farms in the parish, and every bit of land and field was utilised. St John's Nurseries was a new venture and was a row of five very large greenhouses growing tomatoes. It must have been just after four when we paid our driver and tentatively made our way into what seemed like a makeshift office at the side of a tiny farmhouse. We must have looked totally out of place, as we were both dressed to the hilt in suits and ties. We entered, with the phone constantly ringing and met the foreman Dave, a Guernsey man in his late thirties. Beside him was his boss Mr Roy Barette. Always believing honesty was the best policy, we told them what we had done with the telephone box and the cab. They seemed impressed and told us the phone hadn't stopped ringing with applicants. After a few brief questions Mr Barette asked if we could wait outside for a minute. When we were called back in, Dave asked us when we could start. We were to begin our new careers as nurserymen the next afternoon, after collecting our social security cards in the morning.

St John was nearly six miles from St Helier, and our starting time was 8 o'clock. That meant an early morning start and a 30-minute walk to the bus station, then a 30-minute journey. Being young and very fit, we soon got into a routine. On our first afternoon we were warmly welcomed by the staff. They were all local people whose lives seemed to have been spent in the farming industry. Agriculture was still a very big industry back then with the outdoor growth of the famous Jersey Royal potato, and the growing of Jersey tomatoes. That was to be our trade for the summer of 66, helping to grow the Jersey Tom! Ted and Jack were our teachers. Both were in their late sixties, but hard lives made them look much older, and both had been smallholding farmers in their day. They had rented small farms, along with the surrounding fields, and had made a living that had provided the simple basics of life. Hard work was emblazoned on their faces, and their hands and fingers were as tough as leather. They spoke a different language between themselves. Jersey had its own form of French which was described as being a 'Patois.' Most of the words used were French in origin but unlike the smoothness of proper French, Jersey Patois was very guttural and harsh, with English words mixed in. To two English lads it was all very strange, but very amusing. Though educated in very rudimentary parish schools, these were also people who were still able to talk in three languages. French, English, and rubbish! I was to find out that the patois was the first language for the Jerseymen of the farming community, and that St John's still was a busy farming community. For all the hard life that these men had endured we were to find that Jack and Ted were very kind-hearted, and had an inbuilt decency in their character, combined with a good sense of humour. Our hours were long compared to the hours that we would have worked on the mainland. We learned the greenhouses were a new venture and that overtime was on offer. We chose to say yes to it, meaning our average week was 54 hours. We learned more as time went on, but the main thing was that we were young, breathing clean air, mixing in a totally different culture, and enjoying ourselves. It also helped that the cost of living in Jersey was very low, especially tobacco and alcohol. Our foreman was a Guernsey man who had brought his wife and young daughter to Jersey to give his knowledge to the greenhouses since their building completion the previous winter. Dave was another thoroughly decent man in his early 30s and was an expert on tomato greenhouse growing. His little family were given the accommodation of the small farm at the sites entrance. Ted's wife also worked a few hours as did two other local ladies. Unfortunately, another of the staff was a surly Frenchman who seemed to be a general odd job man for the boss, and lived in meagre accommodation in the boss's barn. He made it very obvious he didn't like the English. He was only in his mid-twenties but was of dubious character. At that time there were some French who came to Jersey to escape the law, and he may well have been one of those characters. He always seemed to be banging something or dragging something, as if he had something to prove. He always had a Gauloise cigarette in his mouth and was constantly muttering under his breath in French. His mumbling was often aimed at both Eric and me, and he made his feelings plain that he did not want us there. He took long steps in his 'wellies,' and his clothes, like him, were unkempt and dirty. He reminded me of some hillbilly character from a western, illiterate and ignorant. We were told that he knew English but if he needed to speak to us it was a snide grunt in French. Thankfully he was more so employed down on the main farm, and we were able to give him a wide berth. The main farm of our boss was further down the lane and the glasshouses had been built on one of the farms larger fields. Our jobs were fairly menial, as well as the picking of the tomatoes, each plant had to be trimmed to keep it orderly on the wires that formed the long plant rows. You would continuously work your way up and down the rows from greenhouse to greenhouse throughout the week. I guess it sounds boring, but the sunny days of early summer shone through the glass and fairly soon we were both as brown as berries .There was always a radio on, and it was tuned to the music of the day, so The Beatles and all the other great sixties music helped make the days go quicker. There was also lots of chatter as we learned of our work friends' lives, or we told them of ours. Occasionally our boss Mr Barette would show his face, and he was always smiling and polite, and having a joke in Jersey French. For the most part however, it was Dave who oversaw everything, and he knew all there was to know. The weeks passed, and our lives fell into a pattern. Obviously we were young and wanted to enjoy our freedom, but we kept the weekends for any nights out. We lived on the edge of town and handily there was a cinema at the end of our road. One film I remember vividly starred a young man I had not seen before named Dustin Hoffman. After his appearance in The

Graduate, he never looked back. As our accommodation was sleeping only, we had to eat out. If there was one thing about Eric that I found irritating it was the orderly fashion he liked to run his life, especially when it came to our evening meal. If it was Monday he liked to eat at that cafe, on Tuesdays it would have to be that cafe, and so on through the week. Fortunately, we found a place we both liked called 'Papa's'. For three shillings and sixpence Papa would serve you a soup starter, followed by your main course of meat, two veg and gravy, then your meal concluded with jam roly-poly and custard, and of course a large mug of tea. It never varied, but it was good English grub, and all served at your table by the elderly gent everyone knew as Papa. Eric was just as orderly with his dress, but I guess I shouldn't fault him on that as I too liked to look dapper. I guess living together, working together, and going out of a night together was a lot to ask of two 19-year-old lads, and the bubble was bound to burst, but I will write about that later.

On certain working days (I think it was twice a week) Eric was sent to the packing shed where he worked alongside the boss's wife Eileen. With his London banter he got along well with Eileen and whoever else had been brought in to pack the tomatoes in their small square wooden boxes ready for export .We were to learn that as well as her duties with all the paperwork and packing, Eileen also took visitors at the large farm where she and the boss lived down the lane. She would have the same families coming year after year, serving them bed, breakfast, and an evening meal. All those country folk were what I would call grafters, very hard-working people who asked nothing from anyone. I liked that. It reminded me of my parents, and I've tried to aspire to that same set of principles throughout my life, hating the word debt.

We used to get an hour's lunch break and if the weather was hot, we would make our way to the nearby harbour known as Bonne Nuit Bay (Goodnight Bay). It was at the bottom of a very steep and long hill. I find it hard to believe it now, but we would go down to the bay, have a swim, and march back up the long and steep hill all within one hour. We were however nineteen, fit, and very determined.

Our weekends were quite boozy, but there again we were young, away from home, and out for fun. Fun obviously involved the opposite sex, and I will merely say that we are only nineteen once! My Garston mate Neil arrived in Jersey in the early summer. He got on well with Eric, but Neil was, and still is, the kind of man who gets on with everybody.

It seems almost as if it didn't happen, but Jersey had 'live' music in almost every bar, and there was no shortage of bars! I had taken my 12-string guitar with me, but it never entered my head that I could ever get up and sing and play to an audience. So, our little sleeping only bedroom was as far as my 12-stringer ever got. Funny, but I have just remembered learning and playing the intro to 'Mr Tambourine Man' the Bob Dylan song done by The Byrds on my single bed in that pokey bedroom.

One day we were asked if we could help the Frenchmen lay some concrete for a driveway that would allow vehicles to drive up to the glasshouses. It was obviously going to be quite a job, but we didn't mind, it was something different and we were fit and healthy. The sun beat down on our brown torsos as it was explained by Dave the foreman that our job would be to keep the mixer fed with an appropriate mix of sand, water, cement and aggregate. He gave a demonstration of the different quantities of each to use, and away we went. The Frenchman looked at us as if we were something he had scraped off his wellies, and it was him, armed with a spirit level and plank of wood that we would be supplying the concrete to for the foreseeable future. It was obvious that he didn't think we would be up to the task. I can still hear him now shouting 'More concrete! "More concrete!' He got his concrete, and we built up our muscles. I can't recall how long it took us to complete the roadway, but I know that it was top notch, and the consistency of the concrete was always perfect.

One morning we two English boys, who thought of ourselves as being fit, were really to have our strength tested. It was a beautiful sunny day, and we were informed that Mr Barette needed us to help load up the hay from one of his fields. I think we were quite excited with the idea; it sounded fun and would add to our stories to tell. He duly arrived driving his small Massey Ferguson tractor complete with a trailer on the back which we were told to jump on. We were driven to one of the larger fields further down the lane. All the hay was baled and lying in dozens of rows. The bales looked bigger than we had thought they would be, but we were confident we could do what was required.

Our unfriendly Frenchman, who we had nicknamed 'Powerful Pierre,' was waiting for us. He threw us both a long pitcher each and smirked. Without breaking into a sweat, he put his pitcher into a bale and expertly swung it onto the trailer where Mr Barette was going to stack them in neat rows. I think both the Frenchman and Mr Barette were grinning at our initial feeble attempts to emulate 'Powerful Pierres' expert swing. Those bales were extremely heavy! Gradually we got the hang of it, but it wasn't a job for the weak. The snag of course was that the more bales you put on the trailer, the higher it got, and the more difficult it became, but we endured! It was almost as if we weren't going to let that illiterate Frenchman get the better of us. Once the trailer was loaded the boss would drive up the lane with us walking behind. His farm was a few hundred yards, and we had to start all over again getting the bales into the loft of the farmyard barn. I think without a shadow of a doubt that was the hardest day's work I have done in my entire life, and that my arms and shoulder muscles were crying. The main thing to Eric and myself was that we were able to keep up with "Powerful Pierre." We weren't going to let a hillbilly Frenchman get the better of us.

Every single minute of the day was spent with Eric, so something was bound to snap. I felt guilty if I was meeting a girl, and he was getting letters from his mother saying she was ill. 'Go home, I'll be ok.' I would tell him. If the truth be known he was getting on my nerves and cramping my love life. He was becoming morose, and was obviously upset at the letters his mother was sending him. I asked him if he would mind if I got my mam to call on her to see how ill she was. They didn't know each other, but I knew my mam would do so. At first, he said no, but when I kept telling him he should go home, he reluctantly agreed. By this time, I just wanted to see the back of him. Furnished with Eric's mothers address my mam caught a bus to the Nags Head, Holloway, found the house, and rang the bell. Surprise, surprise! Eric's mother was as fit as a butcher's dog! It was all a ploy to get her baby boy back home. It was as simple as that. For over a month I had been living for twenty-four hours a day, seven days a week with someone who was always miserable. 'Go home,' I kept telling him, 'Go home.' I couldn't say run to your little mummy, but I'd had enough and just wanted him gone. He was adamant that he would stick it out till September. It was almost as if it would be an admittance of defeat to return home, but by that time I just wanted him gone. He was no longer wanting to be in Jersey, but he just wouldn't admit it. He had become antagonistic and surly towards me, and it wasn't pleasant.

Sundays in Jersey meant the Tropicana Bar on the Five Mile Road at St Ouen's Bay. It was THE place to go, and being the sixties, hitch hiking was your form of travel to get there. Hitchhiking seems to have become a thing of the past today, but it was common practice back then. People have become wearier of allowing strangers in their cars, and I guess we were all a lot more trusting and innocent back then. Anyway, the bus service on Sundays was almost non-existent, and a thumb in the air usually did the trick. The Trop, as we called it, was the meeting place for the island's seasonal workers each Sunday afternoon. What made it popular was that it had a disc jockey, something of a rarity in 1966. 'Mick the Mod' sat in a small back room blasting out the hits of the day, and '66 was certainly a great year for British and American records. On this particular Sunday, Eric had been quite surly and stand offish, and there was a definite tension between us. One thing led to another whilst, some words were said and within minutes we were on the sand dunes across the road battering hell out of each other. The fight lasted well over five minutes till we didn't have the strength to throw another punch. Covered in blood, we had got rid of all our built-up tensions. We both felt better for the release of all the weeks of built-up emotions. I cannot remember what we did afterwards. We would certainly not have been allowed back in the Tropicana, as the blood covered both our faces and our clothes. Anyway, we got back to town, and the matter was never discussed again, but he still wouldn't go home!

MY JERSEY GIRL

One day in late July a tiny and pretty girl appeared at the greenhouse. She had a pleasant demeanour and obviously knew all the staff. She looked my way with the kind of smile I can still recall over half a century later. She didn't stay long, and after she had gone, I was told she was Mr Barette's daughter who was back home for the summer break from college in England. I thought to myself, this girl is out of my league, not only is she brainy, but she's the boss's daughter! I decided to remain aloof and keep my distance. However, she kept coming back each day and made it very plain that she had set her eyes on me. It was whilst she was making one of her greenhouse visits that my trimming knife slipped and I made a deep cut into my forefinger. She came to my aid spontaneously and led me out to the boiler house where the medical box was. Sat me down and tended my wound in the gentlest of ways. We talked as if we had known each other all our lives, she had such a lovely sense of humour and it all just felt so natural. I was very hesitant to ask the boss's daughter out, but it became obvious that we had a mutual bond. Once more fate, or my lucky angel, was looking after me. That Saturday night June Amy Barette borrowed her dads Morris Oxford estate, picked me up, and prior to going out to one of the islands many cabarets, took me to her parents' farm. It was the last place on earth I wanted to go but I think she did it deliberately to put my mind at rest. I had never been into the main farm, and although I found Mr Barette to be very pleasant, he was my boss, and I kept my distance out of respect. June led me into a very sparse and tiny kitchen diner and sat me down at a table that covered most of the floor space. I was surprised at how spartan it was, and it certainly was anything but grand. Just then Mr Barette entered through a door from the main house. He had no shirt over his white singlet and was not wearing his false teeth. I guess I realised there and then that these were ordinary people and that I had the seal of approval. We had a wonderful evening at one of Jersey's many cabaret shows and even won a huge toy cat in the raffle.

We became almost inseparable during that late summer of 1966. I left Eric to get on with it. If it was his choice to stay, then he had to accept that I had a life, and was going to live it. He wasn't completely left out however, and joined us on several occasions. We have all heard that holiday romances do not last, but I think we both were aware that what we had was special. It did not alter the fact however that June had one more year at college in Newcastle, and I was returning to London. We had seven weeks, and then we would face the reality of being hundreds of miles apart. We packed so much in during the brief time we had together, each day becoming more fond of each other. She always seemed to be able to borrow her dad's car, so was able to show me places I had not known of or seen in the beautiful island she was so proud of. We were both interested in history, and she taught me so much of the islands recent and distant past. Its association with William the Conqueror, the Norman conquest of Britain, and the five years Jersey had spent under German occupation just over twenty years before. June told me of her parents' background and the profound effect that the war had on their lives.

It was 1940 and Hitler's armies had literally swept through Europe. By mid-June they had taken possession of Paris. Being just eighteen miles from the Normandy coast, it was obvious that The Channel Islands were next. Being of no strategic value, Churchill decided that they were undefendable. The islands were demilitarised and all military personnel taken to England. Islanders were given the option of leaving for England or staying. Ships were duly sent to the islands and those wishing to leave were evacuated and scattered across the U.K. June's grandfather had seven children, six boys and one daughter. They resided in St Helier, where Joseph Barette ran a successful potato and tomato export business. He made the decision that his family would stay and face whatever fate had in store. He had been raised within a farming background, and there was still the family farm in the extreme north of the island. Fearing for the safety of his wife and children, he decided it would be safer to get away from the main populated area and move his family out to the country. Realising that there would be food shortages under an occupation, he knew the farm put his family in a far better position. On June 28th nine German Heinkel aircrafts bombed and machine gunned the St Helier harbour area leaving ten civilians dead. By all accounts the Germans were unaware that the islands had been cleared of all military manpower, a sad error on the part of the British government. An ultimatum was issued that white flags be flown, and white crosses be painted on the ground. Three days later the official occupation began. It was to last five years, and the coast of the west of Jersey would be turned into one of the most fortified regions of Europe. Normality had gone for the Barette family, especially for eldest son Roy. Being a teenager, he had been robbed of his youth and became very staunch in his hatred for the occupiers of his island. Though the islands served no military advantage to the Germans, Hitler saw them as an important propaganda exercise. German cameramen took full advantage of trying to purvey an image of harmony and tranquillity and there is a famous piece of film (shot in Guernsey) showed a uniformed policeman chauffeuring then opening the car door for a German officer. Other film taken shows a military band marching through the streets of St Helier. Taking film of all things British, usually with soldiers and islanders sharing St Helier streets was shown to German cinema audiences giving the impression that the English mainland would soon follow suit.

The governing of the island was placed under German rule with the Jersey Bailiff as its figurehead. Curfews were introduced, the Freemason Temple was closed, radios were made illegal, and the one and only newspaper placed under strict censorship. It was hard on Roy Barette to see some of the women in St John fraternising with the Germans and they acquired the nickname 'Jerry-bags'. There wasn't much one could do about such women other than treat them with contempt, but Roy and several mates would paint V for victory signs on their doors. Such acts could not only lead to prison, but also to prison in occupied France. It wasn't just the women who fraternised, some farmers were also over friendly with the island's foreign masters. All those people would be remembered and would face retribution after the war in one way or another.

For reasons best known to himself, Hitler seemed to believe that the British would invade the occupied islands. He therefore gave orders to make them impregnable from Allied invasion. Plans were drawn up to lay thousands of mines on the western facing beaches, the only part of Jersey that had good flat access to landing craft. As he was about to do across the whole of the western coasts of Europe, he wanted the islands to be an extension of what would become known as the Atlantic wall. Such a massive undertaking entailed bunkers, pillboxes, gun turrets and a massive strengthening of the sea walls. Labour for such an enterprise would be made up of forced workers from France. Hundreds of unemployed Algerian and Moroccans were shipped in, having been given by the Vichy government to the Germans. Over 2000 Spanish political prisoners also arrived (opponents of Franco who had escaped into France) as well as many Frenchmen and Belgians. All were to suffer great deprivation, but none were treated so cruelly as the Russians and Ukrainians that followed later. The main pub in St Johns was the hotel in the main area of the parish, near to the school, the parish church, and the parish hall. It was commandeered by The Organization Todt (Hitler's Civil and Engineering Organisation), and its grounds and main building were used to accommodate the east European Slavs, people the Germans thought of a sub-human. Those slave workers, some of whom had been made to walk the full breadth of Europe were visible to parishioners. Their appearance and physical condition made it perfectly clear to all that the Germans were a cruel and brutal enemy.

Growing up and seeing such sights had a lasting effect on Roy Barrett. Fortunately, he was finding out that farming was his niche, and he knew that it was how he wanted to spend his life. There was another thing in Roy's life that was making the unpleasantness of occupation more tolerable, a girl by the name of Eileen. Two hundred yards further up the lane from the farm was a corner shop owned and run by Mr and Mrs Stanley Amy. They had two daughters, and Eileen would become the love of Roy's life. There is much more I could write of the war, but I will conclude the episode by writing that at war's end Roy and Eileen had married, and that Roy remained as a St John's farmer. The decade that followed the war was good for the Jersey farmer with the popularity of the unique Jersey Royal potato. Tourism to the island grew also, due to strong ferry ties with England. Eileen, though working full time on the farm, started taking in visitors at the farm, many of whom would come back year after year. Roy also went on to become a staunch advocate of the honorary service and enrolled using the normal route as an honorary police officer. By 1966, he had become a Centenier (Chief of Police).

So that was the background that June had been born into in 1946.She had been raised on a farm on an island eighteen miles from the Normandy coast, where her parents had just been liberated after five years of occupation, and whose first language was Jersey patois. June's knowledge of English was limited until she started to attend the local parish infants' school, and her social life was to be limited and centred around visits to the parish Methodist church. Her background could not have been more different from mine, yet something had brought us together that made such things irrelevant. September arrived. Our summer together was over, and the real test of our relationship was to be put to the test.

THE NIGHT TRAIN TO NEWCASTLE

British Rail as it was then known, was in the final years of its steam age in 1966. Nationalised by the Labour government just after the war, the rail industry was owned by the taxpayers of Britain. Each Friday night there was an overnight service from Kings Cross to Newcastle. It was to be the train I constantly used throughout the winter of 1966, up to the summer of 1967.

London, September 1966

Having returned to London 1 was able to get my job back at Mac Fisheries. There was no shortage of overtime which suited me because train trips to Newcastle were not going to be cheap, and being a journey of nearly 300 miles, 1 had never contemplated doing it by coach. June had begun her final year at teachers training college, and we were writing to each other every day, only phoning when essential. She came to London first for an Autumn weekend trip, accompanied by two of her college friends. Uncle Bryan was on the scene at that time and kindly obliged by providing overnight accommodation for them. It's a long time ago, but 1 think we all had a tourist type sightseeing weekend. After that it was mainly me travelling up north on Friday nights and returning on the overnight train on the Sunday evening. June found me accommodation at a very basic bed and breakfast near her college. The phrase 'very basic' was apt because the landlady had failed to inform me that l was not only sharing a room but was sharing a double bed with another of her clients! Having spent a great evening out with June and another couple, I had returned to my B&B, exhausted having travelled up the previous night on the train with very little sleep. I immediately went straight to bed and turned the light off and fell into a deep sleep. Whoever the gentleman was, he never turned the light on, and I was not awoken until he was in the bed with me! I can't remember too much about that night other than it was the longest of my life. Having paid for my long night in advance, I was up and out of the premises shortly after six the next morning. Cold but relieved, I found a park nearby and sat and dozed on a bench. As soon as I was able (it being a Sunday morning) I found myself in a 'greasy spoon' cafe and had a Full English! Needless to say, another B&B was found for my next visit. That was how we continued our romance for the next year, travelling up and down the country.

Newcastle was the perfect place for a girl like June to see that life wasn't easy for working class people. She had enjoyed a sheltered life on an island and had never known the meaning of deprivation. She told me she learned the importance of the free school milk for some children, it being the only sustenance they got in the morning. She also told me that some of her pupils had mothers who had lowered themselves into prostitution to give their kids a chance. Her Newcastle experience had opened her eyes and was to make her a far more caring teacher in years to come. I have one overriding memory of her college. It was a Sunday evening on the 25th of June in 1967. Normally I would not have been in Newcastle on a Sunday night, but on a train, however this night was special. The whole country wanted to see the first global T.V. link show Our World, which was going to feature a new Beatles song performed 'live' in Abbey Road Studios. Most of the college, including many tutors, were packed into the hall to witness history. No one was disappointed to hear John Lennon telling the 50,000,000 worldwide viewers that 'All you need is love.'

June informed me that she had a year to teach in England before being able to apply for a post in Jersey. We discussed it and of course we wanted to be near each other. She was successful in an application she had made to a Juniors school in Mill Hill, a pleasant area only three stops away from Archway Underground Station. That one year turned into two years!

We found a two room flat nearby to Pemberton

Gardens, it was clean, the tenants were all girls of a similar age, and the landlady lived within the very large house. By this time, we had reached agreement to vigorously save out money and marry and settle in Jersey. I felt that I had much to prove to June's parents that I was the right man for their daughter. I therefore wanted to return to Jersey with money in my pocket, Mac Fisheries always provided the opportunity for overtime, and I soon got into the regime of working six nights a week. It was good to know that June enjoyed her school, and I was pleased that she was in a pleasant low crime suburban area. Saving our money didn't mean not going out as London is still a city where so much is still free and interesting. We both enjoyed history, and London is a fascinating place for such an interest. We were also able to make up a foursome. I have   forgotten where I met Tommy, but he was a lad of the same age who lived nearby and played guitar and liked country music. His parents were Polish and had a newsagents shop in Holloway Road. Somehow at an earlier time we had become friendly, and he had a girlfriend named Jill. We teamed up as a foursome, and luckily Jill and June hit it off. We became almost inseparable at weekends. Tommy was one of those young lads who always placed importance in having a car, which greatly helped his relationship with Jill, who lived ten miles away in Borehamwood. We all got on very well and spent 1968 having fun and enjoying being young. I had a reel-to-reel tape recorder, and we would get together in Pemberton Gardens and play songs and record them. I would love to have those recordings, but the tape recorder, and a lot of other things, got lost along the way. I was Tommy's best man, but sadly their marriage broke up, and we lost Jill for many years. Happily, we found each other in the 1990's and she now lives happily with her husband Derek in Broadstairs. We are still in regular contact and she remains a valued friend. During all this period I had always kept in touch with Neil in Garston. He was my mucker, and though we were separated by the miles our friendship was always there in times of importance and need. Besides he too was in a relationship, so there were other priorities. I joined June in Jersey in the August of 1969, as she had returned home earlier. We had said our goodbyes to England, we were engaged, and Jersey was to be our home.

JERSEY

August 1969

I arrived in the island with £3,000 in my bank account. That was a great deal of money in 1969.I had been doing lots of overtime (six nights per week) during the previous two years. I wanted, in the only way I knew how, to show June's parents that I was a reliable and hardworking man. I never felt that June's mother completely accepted me, which I guess was understandable. If I said white, she said black. Luckily, I was thick skinned, and knew that given time I could bring her around. It was a very different world back then, and Jersey country people in many ways lived isolated lives that revolved almost totally within the confines of their island parish. Some of those country folk were suspicious of outsiders, and I guess to Eileen I was still an outsider. I had no such difficulties with June's dad, who treated me with nothing other than respect, and acceptance. He was a highly educated man, well read, and worldly wise. June and her father were very close alike, and I think he trusted her judgement. I more than proved my worth to Eileen in the decades that followed.

I was housed just up the lane from the farm with June's grandparents, where I had the sheer joy of sleeping in a feather bed. Since the 193s, or possibly before, they had owned a country shop that sold all the basics required for the locals. They had just retired, and Mr Stanley George Amy and his wife Elsie May had sold the property and moved a few doors up into one of the three cottages that Stan had built prior to the war, Stan having been a master carpenter by trade. The ethic of Stan and Elsie was hard work, and that's how they had lived their lives. I liked them both very much and we got on well. Stan liked a tipple, but it never affected his ability for hard work, and he was always engaged in some job or other.

June had been accepted into a local country junior school, and I got several different unremarkable jobs which helped our assets. We had arranged to marry in the late March of the coming year. Unbeknown to me, June and her dad were trying to get permission for him to give us a small plot of land to build on. The island authorities were very strict on giving permission to build on green zones, and all the plots that Roy thought suitable were in the green zone. Prior to our marriage we were able to rent a cottage on the outskirts of St Helier. The marriage was held in the local parish church, with my family in attendance, and we honeymooned in Benidorm. Benidorm was not the huge bustling tourist attraction that it is today, but it was obvious what direction it was heading as much of it could best be described as a building site. On our return we slipped into married life with ease and even got ourselves a cat! Stan and Elsie also had land, and it was then that June told me that they too were trying to help us with the gift of a plot. It was all too much for an Englishman like me to take in. Such kindness was unknown to me, and I thought it best to say little and keep a low profile. The island authorities at that time had a system whereby young couples (who had plots) could apply for what was known as a States Loan. Basically, it was a mortgage of up to 40 years, at a set rate that would never increase in its duration. Looking back, it was a unique opportunity for couples, which sadly was withdrawn some years later. June's grandparents had also utilized their land by growing Jersey's famous Jersey Royals. Their small fields were on the headland on top of the cliffs and were renowned for getting an early crop. The earlier the better, as the new potato was always top range and good money could be made. In the 1930s Stan had built a large, corrugated iron shed for the storage of his potato seeds and field equipment. By 1970 the shed was the worse for wear and unsightly and was also in a tiny unusable field. An application was made to what was known then as The Island Development Committee to remove the shed and build a bungalow on its approximate site. The application, much to our surprise, was granted. We then went through the motions of getting an architect to design us a bungalow. Here again I cannot stress the kindness of friends. June's best friend from her school days was married to an architect, and he drew up a plan for us for a total cost of nothing! It was submitted and passed. All this was difficult for a kid from 'under the bridge' to take in, but I was determined to show that I was worthy of such kindness. Tenders were put out to builders, and we chose a local man whose work we had seen and admired.

My first taste of tragedy hit in May 1971. The greenhouse produce of tomatoes had altered a few years before to the growing of chrysanthemums. This was due to the water supply which was found to be contaminated. My father-in-law Roy was delivering a consignment of flowers to the St Helier market when he had a massive heart attack. His death was immediate, and he was aged just 44. His relationship with Eileen had been a joy to behold. They were besotted with each other, and she was going to be left a widow, at the young age of 42. It was heartbreaking. She had been his right hand and supported him in all he did. Roy was proud of the service he was able to give in his role as centenier. There is no doubt that he would have gone on to become the Constable of the parish, its highest accolade. I was later asked to carry Roy's coffin, an honour that proved I was gaining acceptance to Eileen. Roy's loss hit June badly as he had been on the same intellectual level in their mutual interests. We both assured Eileen that we were there for her, and she would be our number one priority of in days to come, a promise we more than lived up to.

At the same time our bungalow had begun. The things that were all very new and very strange to me. I was taking on responsibilities and had become the male figure in our family unit of having a mortgage and watching our very own bungalow being built. Everything seemed to go up so quickly and then came to a full stop. The plumber would be waiting on the electrician, the electrician would have to finish his other job, then the plumber had to wait for some parts from the U.K. Our bungalow was completed in 1971.There were many things missing when we moved in, but we were of one mind that we would only purchase that which we could afford. So, several rooms were without carpets, with just the bare concrete the builder had left, I remember our first black and white T.V., it was a second hand one I bought it from a guy I worked with. We got there eventually, but most importantly for us, we had no debts. The patch that we had built on was in a very poor condition, with much building mess left. So began a job that was going to take me over a quarter of a century, I knew nothing of gardening, but I had a point to prove that I was going to repay June's family for the trust they placed in me. I would do so by creating a special garden to be proud of. We were very lucky to have a French couple living in a cottage next door, and Mr and Mrs Le Manach were a great help to both June and me. Our first child was born during the summer heat waves of 1972. June was never a great one for such weather and Joanna Jane came as a blessing and relief in more ways than one. There is no explaining to anyone the joy I felt in my life. Every step I took seemed to have been the right step.

Being a loving couple, living in a new bungalow in the beautiful Jersey countryside, and being given the gift of a baby girl, it was like a fairytale.

MUSIC, MONEY, AND TRAVEL

1972 saw me finding employment as a sales representative for a long-established family business in the booming tourist industry. As well as trying to find new business, I also had a list of dozens of regular clients to call on each week. I never envisioned being a salesman, as I have always thought of myself as being quite reserved. Yet I had beaten dozens of others who had applied for the job, so I must have had something going for me. I desperately wanted stability in my new life, and it was a well-respected company, and there was commission to be earned. Handed down from father to son, the company had been in business since 1842 and had a small factory that produced all kinds of pipe and hand rolling tobaccos. The premises overlooked the harbour in St Helier and had the most interesting photos of the company's history. Pictured were sailing ships that had brought tobaccos from across the globe to be blended and packaged. They would then be exported to Europe and America. For a small company the generational family members had built up a very good international business. They also had a lot of agencies, including top brand cigarettes and cigars, as well as selling virtually anything that would appeal to tourists. Though I never truly felt comfortable being a salesman, I built up a trust with my customers and seemed to be liked. I stayed with them for 25 years until tourism declined and then joined the island electricity company for the last 15 years of my working life.

June felt strongly that she wanted to devote the first few years of Joanna's life as a full-time mother, so she temporarily opted out of teaching. She acquired an evening job having women's clothes parties, whilst I baby sat. It was during this period that we had been invited to a party of one of her teaching friends. Our social life had all but disappeared due to lack of funds and baby duties, so we saw it as a chance to get out the house. Teachers have a habit of talking shop, and this get-together was to be no different. I smiled a lot and tried to mingle but found it all a bit of a strain. Then two men of the party started playing guitars. These were the kind of occasions I had grown up with, sitting in on a party and having a sing along. I waited a while until they had done what seemed to be their repertoire then approached and asked if I could borrow one of their guitars. I don't think I was being greedy, but that guitar stayed in my hand for the rest of the night, and I had no objections from anybody. The songs were all basic three or four chord stuff, but people seemed to have enjoyed it. At the end of the night I learned that one half of the duo was a successful businessman and belonged to a family that owned all the major dry-cleaning shops in

Jersey and Guernsey. He was adamant that we mustn't just end the night without making arrangements to meet again. I thought no more of it until sometime later I was informed that Graham, that was the businessman's name, had been and spent hundreds of pounds on amplifiers and microphones etc. He had also found a drummer and was deadly serious about us actually becoming a group. It was all a lot for me to take in, having just played mainly for myself or at someone's party. I agreed to meet up and see where it led. To cut a long story short I was then informed that Graham had arranged a meeting with the owners of a new music pub at St Ouen's Bay. I felt I was being pushed into something I was not prepared for, but Graham had a way that could charm the birds off the trees. What made the Sable D'or different from other venues was that families could spend the night together in the main lounge. At that time Jersey laws were very strict on children's admittance into pubs. The law said they could not be in a room with a bar. The two brothers that had built the venue had gotten around the law by building hatches from the bar area, into the music lounge. The customer would go to the hatches for service, therefore not breaking the rules.

From what I can remember (it was half a century ago) we had a few weeks to practice and then would be playing three nights a week. I soon found out that the onus was on me to come up with a programme. Over time that programme extended, but the onus always remained with me. If I was going to be the front man, then it had to be as good as possible. I know I was often rude and a hard taskmaster, but we must have been doing something right as we were pulling in good numbers. So, there I was! The husband in a loving marriage, the daddy to a sweet little baby girl, the owner of a bungalow built on top of a cliff, and a semi professional musician. The cream on the cake was the arrival of Stephen in 1975, a son I could turn into an avid Liverpool supporter like myself! Someone or something was truly looking after me. I felt like a million dollars. I left the Sable D'or after about eighteen months and joined other musicians at another venue further up the bay. In the years that followed I either worked with others or on my own in hotels and pubs. I was lucky enough to have worked a few years with Cyril, a pedal steel guitarist who taught me jazz chords, so I was learning and expanding my musical capabilities. That improvement meant I was capable of catering for events like private dinner/dances. I would like to believe that during those hectic days and nights that I was still a good and caring dad, as I was certainly a proud one. As it was in my childhood, Sunday was always sacrosanct and was kept as a family day.

I had created a lovely front garden during the

seventies, and it was a pastime that brought me a great deal of pleasure. It was extremely hard work as being on a cliff the ground was full of granite. I asked for, and received, no help from anyone. I felt it was my way of saying thank you for the life I had been given. After the loss of my father-in-law Eileen had accepted herself as a widow, and though only 42, never had thoughts of remarrying. She had many friends in the farming community, and June and I would often join them for parochial gatherings and day trips to France. That generation of Jersey country folk were good hard-working people, and luckily, I got on very well with them. Yes, the 'mudman' had travelled a long way, but Liverpool was always with him. Neil had married, and he and Pat would come to Jersey during the summers and stay with us. June and I would also visit and stay with them in Liverpool. Sadly, the city was going through hard times, but not with its football! I took my 4'11''inch Jersey girl into the Kop during the time of Shankly and we were able to see great players like Keegan, Kennedy, and Heighway destroy Bolton 3-0.We proudly sang 'You'll never walk alone' and saw the man who created one of the best and most successful clubs in Europe. June had loved her football since childhood, when her dad was goalkeeper for the parish team. They even made her the team mascot.

I was doing a gig in a private hotel in the season of

1981 when at breaktime I was approached by two men who had sat quietly listening to my vocal efforts. They told me they were going to start a country music club and asked if I could get a band organized. A John Travolta movie 'Urban Cowboy' had apparently been very successful on both sides of the Atlantic. It featured line dancing and had started a craze both in America and the U.K. with many clubs opening. I knew I could muster up a band, but wasn't sure I wanted to get involved with the cowboy and cowgirl aspect. To me that image of brash western apparel that rightly put people off Country Music. It gave a Hollywood image of cowboys like Roy Rogers. My taste were artists like Kris Kristofferson, Willie Nelson, Johnny Cash, and Waylon Jennings whose music delved into other genres, often with lyrics that could be controversial and touch a nerve. They had also never allowed themselves to be slotted into what had become the overproduced and silky 'Nashville Sound.'

I told them that I could get a band, money was discussed and agreed, and several weeks later The Jersey Country Music Club began. By that time BBC local radio had opened, so there was lots of free advertising for the opening night. Band members were all guys I'd worked with previously and the venue was full. So began a decade of regular work.

The Wolf's Caves had opened as a pub with one of

the most panoramic views in Jersey, and its claim to fame was that it had the longest bar in the island. It overlooked the north headland with beautiful views of the Normandy coast. Fortunately for me, it was just around the corner from our bungalow. I knew Martin the manager, as he had run a pub in town that was frequented by Liverpool lads, several of whom were Garstonians. The brewery that had built the pub had done so with no fanfare, and with the bare minimum of expense. Indeed, it lacked important things like a decent size kitchen to enable the sale of meals. The main room was huge but had inadequate heating. Being off the beaten track there was also no connection to mains water, so the building was reliant on a well that frequently went dry. Martin's young family lived on the premises, but such was the thinness of the walls that any 'live' music' made their lives very uncomfortable. I had done quite a few dinner / dances at the venue, but the room never felt warm. I felt sorry for Martin, as he struggled with problems that could so easily have been prevented had the owners been a little less thrifty.

To me, The Wolf's Caves would be the perfect venue. The summer season lay ahead, and a very large venue with fabulous views would bring in tourists. It would also put some life into a pub that had everything going for it but needed a jolt. I approached Martin, who for obvious reasons of his family's comfort was sceptical, but who eventually agreed. In the first year the club played to full houses. One night a week extended to three, so there was no need for me to work elsewhere. The club also managed to get a sponsorship from the agents of Marlboro cigarettes and changed its name to The Marlboro Country Music Club. The extra revenue allowed the club to bring British and American artists to the island.

One club night while setting up my musical gear, a lad in his twenties came in and introduced himself. I immediately cottoned on to a scouse accent. I had seen 'Slick Mick' working in The Devils Hole, a pub in the next parish, but had no idea of his musical talent. He asked me if I would mind him bringing his piano in and sitting in with the band. A scouser, a piano player, I couldn't believe my luck. From the first number I knew I must hang on to this young man. Not only did he play piano, but he had a trained harmony voice, and with no rehearsals he was right there. His musical ability was phenomenal, and to top it all he knew the words of most of the songs. I had the good fortune to play alongside Mick for five years during which we became great friends, a relationship that carries on to this day. We even bought a boat together and shared many laughs fishing off Bonne Nuit. Whilst in Jersey, he took a course on the Open University that eventually led to a career of teaching music at a secondary school in

Dublin. He recently retired, and we regularly meet up in Liverpool. Music was never as enjoyable without Mick and after he departed, I was just going through the motions, and the enjoyment was beginning to fade.

June and I made our first visit to the U.S.A. in 1981. Trans-Atlantic flights had drastically dropped their prices due to Freddie Laker, an English airline entrepreneur. Way ahead of his time, he got permission to introduce cheap flights to New York, in the face of the powerful monopoly companies. Eventually those large monopolies fell into competition with one another and made America accessible to ordinary Europeans.

I spent months on the planning of our first self-drive Stateside vacation. Due to June's fear of the large cities, I worked on a route that would take us to the more rural and tranquil parts of the south. Because June was a teacher our trip would have to be in the August, and we were to learn just how hot and sultry the southern states could be. It did not however spoil what was to be the first of many such off the track American adventures. Our journey took us on a circular route from Atlanta in Georgia up to North Carolina, Tennessee, and Alabama. It was music all the way, especially in Nashville. We took our kids on one of the next trips and introduced them to the coastline of California. In the years that followed, aided by the money I was earning playing music, I planned and drove thousands of miles through states like Washington, Idaho, Montana, Wyoming, Arizona, Utah, Colorado and Nevada. The kids joined us for trips that were more family orientated in Florida, L.A. and New York. We made some good friends also, who came and stayed with us in Jersey. Because of the post war world I was born into, all things American were dreamlike, and the little kid who had sat open mouthed in The Garston Empire looking up to the big Cinemascope screen, had turned his dreams into reality on the highways and byways of the 'real' America.

We watched our children grow. They were good kids and never caused us any problems. Joanna followed in her mother's footsteps by becoming a teacher. Like her mother, she was also an avid netball player. Stephen was a good footballer and represented the island several times. Like his dad he became a Liverpool fanatic and is a successful businessman. I am extremely proud of my children who are both happily married and have given me the great joy of three adorable granddaughters.

It became obvious in the nineties that Jersey was changing. Tourism was declining due to governmental neglect and cheaper flights to the continent. Hotels were being knocked down or were converted into apartments. Cabarets and musical venues were disappearing. Agriculture saw the loss of the small farmer, who had given way to big, amalgamated groups. The island government had placed finance as its main industry. High wages paid by new finance companies were not matched in the public sector. Huge ugly office buildings were springing up throughout the town, and bit by bit Jersey was losing its character. The island had also become one of the most expensive places in Europe to live. Opportunities for the young had dwindled, and housing prices and rents had skyrocketed.

THE WORST YEAR OF MY LIFE

March 2006

I had entered my 60th year believing there was everything to look forward to. It was all so well planned out. June's early retirement would give her more time to be the loving grandmother she had so looked forward to being. There would be time to plan the holidays we had saved and dreamed of. There would be time for her to get more involved with the island affairs she felt so passionately about. Most importantly, we would just have time to be ourselves, and to take stock of how to spend our last years. Fate, that had been so generous to me, had other plans, and stepped in with an unexpected horror that turned our dreams to oblivion.

On the first day of 2006 at the wonderful age of 94, my mam passed in her sleep. Though it was not entirely unexpected, she was my mother, and her death upset me deeply. The life that had always been on an upward course had taken a downward spiral. Seven weeks after my mams death I lost the girl I had loved since I was 19 in the most horrendous of car accidents. Why? How could something so horrible happen to such a good and giving person? l could not get my brain to process what had happened. 2006 would turn out to be the most awful year of my life, and if l am honest, l have never truly fully recovered. My world was shattered, and a nightmare began that I have never really awoken from. It was no bad dream; it was reality in its most heartbreaking and awful form. You see it was me that found her. It was me who was the first on the scene. I knew that due to a freak accident my 4'11" Jersey girl had left us. I have no wish to go over the awful details, but suffice to say that no one else was involved, and the coroner would later decree that it was 'death by misadventure.' It didn't matter to me what terminology her death was given; she was gone forever.

The cemetery was quiet, and the sun warmed the back of my neck with its rays of an impending Spring. The letter in my hand had been the final one of many I had written the night before in the best handwriting I could muster. I wanted the words within to be clear, concise, and to show the love and depth of my sorrow. I wanted the words to thank her for always seeing the good in me, and for always picking me up when l stumbled. I wanted the words to express my sorrow for the little selfish things I had done during the decades we had shared. There weren't many in number, but they were still stupid and uncalled for. Daft things that she always forgave me for. I wanted to thank her for always looking at me as if I were still the 19-year-old boy she had fallen in love with forty years before. The boy who turned into the man she never doubted. I wanted my letter to say thank you for the life she had given me, so rich, and always with the constant awareness that l was adored. I also wanted the words to convey the pride I held for the two grief-stricken children she had given me. I wanted her to know that l had come to realise that there is nothing richer in life than giving and receiving unquestioned love.

I reached into my pocket for the lighter that was going to help me say the final goodbye that I had been robbed of. My hand trembled and more tears welled up as the letter caught fire. Slowly the ashes fell on the soil beneath which she would lay until the end of time. Trying to avoid the flame, l kept moving the letter round in my hands to ensure that every shred of the paper was burnt. I wanted each private word to be accepted and understood from one soul to another. The previous morning, like all the other depressing mornings I had endured in the past weeks, began early.

Being on compassionate leave from work, and with the warmth of the Spring sunlight beaming over my garden, I decided I must get out somewhere. I drove west to St Ouen's Bay, and the western Jersey coastline that was still rugged and unspoilt by man. After a brief walk on the beach, I entered a cafe that l knew to be rented by an old workmate from many years before. I needed to be amongst people but had forgotten that it was midweek and that it was still early in the year. The cafe only had a few customers, but at least I was out of the house where her memories haunted every room. Tony was nowhere to be seen, so I ordered a coffee with milk and took it to a bench outside. Within minutes he had joined me and sat down. He had been busy in the kitchen but had noticed me through the cafe window. In the previous weeks l had been taken by surprise how dealing with death can be an embarrassment to some people. Of course, I had received dozens of wonderful and heartfelt letters of sympathy, but actual contact with non-family people had been rare. No one rang my doorbell, and the phone calls had come to an abrupt end. People l thought of as friends crossed the street rather than face me. It hurt. I wanted acknowledgement. A simple touch on the arm. A few kind words. Anything to show me they understood.

I found Tony to be the perfect person to just sit and be in the company of. He knew the right words to say and not say, and his sympathies were genuine. Though English in his raising, he had been born in Italy, and I think that his Latin blood had made it easier for him to relate to emotion and the five-letter word the British find difficult to deal with. Like many islanders, Tony had heard of June's tragic and horrific accident in the local media. Coverage had been heavy, with one journalist describing her as 'a daughter of the island.' To me, that was a lovely and true description of June, for she truly loved Jersey, if not always of how it was governed. Tony didn't know June, but we had worked together many years before. He had always had a knowledge of the catering industry and had progressed into acquiring several beach franchises from The States of Jersey. I had once been a salesman and Tony always put business my way. He simply put a hand on my shoulder with no words spoken and sat down opposite me. He seemed to know that I needed to unburden myself and talk of my loss. He sat back and listened without interruption as I tried to explain my inability to come to terms with the harrowing events of the previous month. The horror of it all, and of my regret at not having had the chance to say goodbye. 'There was so much left unsaid,' I told him, brushing yet another tear from my eye.

He made little comment and waited until I ran out of words. 'You need to say goodbye, you need to find yourself, and you have to move on and begin a new life.'

They were words I needed to be told, but those I was in close contact with in the weeks following her death were as deeply traumatised as I was and still looking backwards. Through self-respect and knowing June would not have wanted it otherwise, I had deliberately avoided alcohol or prescription drugs to get me through. I had a duty not just to myself but to my children. It was however very, very hard.

Tony's words were precisely what I needed to be told. I needed to accept that June had gone, and that my own life and health were of greater importance than continually looking backwards. He then told me of a little custom he had heard his mother talk of that could possibly help. He said that I should write down all my feelings in a goodbye letter, take it to her grave and set fire to it. With the ashes on her resting place, and with goodbye words from the heart, it could possibly help me let go. It seemed such a romantic idea, especially coming from someone I had only spoken to in a very different manner. It made a great deal of sense however, as I was in mental turmoil. So, without telling anyone, that night I sat and poured out my heart. I wrote and then discarded page after page of private feelings, of gratitude, of love, and of regret until I satisfied myself that my final goodbye covered all there was to say about our forty years together.

I had never given much thought about the hereafter or God, but I knew June believed. I always felt there was an innate goodness in her, a special characteristic that was instantly recognised by people. It had certainly been recognised by the six hundred people who had forsaken the heavy rain on the day of her funeral. That horrible late winter morning, they had filled the Church to its capacity, yet people kept arriving. A Tannoy speaker relayed the service to a very full congregation in the Parish Hall across the road. Some people, unable to find room in either building, stood outside under umbrellas in the pouring rain. Such was the love and respect she had warranted from people of all walks of life. Hers had been a life of service, and the giving of an education is one of the greatest gifts we mortals can receive. To some, teaching is a job, but to June it was a vocation, and the letters I had received from grateful parents, politicians, ex pupils, work colleagues, relations and friends, confirmed that she was not just appreciated, but had been loved. That love had been showered on me for half a century. After the tragic events of that February I had learned in the most heart wrenching way how blessed I had been, and that my life was never to be the same. Up to that point my existence had been one of continuous growth and good fortune. It was as though fate or whatever entity guides us had said, 'This mortal has had it too good; it's time for him to be taught a lesson.'

After her funeral the phone, which had been so busy with calls of sympathy, suddenly and abruptly, stopped ringing. All the kind friends and relatives who had flown from the mainland had returned to their own lives. For the first time for over three decades, the inside of the bungalow where June and I had made our lives was bereft of laughter, fun, or conversation. Our daughter Jo, who had endured and coped with that awful day so much better than me, had the extra pressure of being the mother of a baby girl, and another girl aged three. Thankfully they lived in the cottage next door so our days could be shared. It was the nights that I was alone that I was at my lowest ebb, talking to myself, and seeing a memory in every room. It was at such a time, almost as if she were there beside me, that I made an oath to mourn for one year. I promised her, and myself, that l would do my best to keep a sound mind, look after myself, my family, and honour her memory. For the next 12 months that is what l did. It wasn't easy as all the plans I had made for the future were with June in mind. 2006 would have been the year she was going to take early retirement. Being the same age, but feeling I needed to keep paying into my work pension, we agreed I should remain at my job for a few more years. The music had died.

I had stopped my evening work as a semi-professional singer/guitarist, which I had done for over 30 years, and we were looking forward to being able to relax more and enjoy doing the normal things and just grow old together. June and I had been given the gift of two lovely granddaughters who would grow up having never known the joy of hearing June's laughter, or of having such a wonderful person as a granny. I would do my best in some small way to fill that void, but of course it was an impossibility.

I had returned to my day job after several weeks leave, and it was as though nothing had happened. I wasn't expecting anyone to put an arm around me, but just a simple few words of sympathy would have sufficed, but I received an evasive silence. I'm still saddened that people find it so hard to relate to others at their time of loss. All I needed was a little touch, or a few words. Admittedly I wasn't particularly close to those I worked with, but I expected much more humanity than l received.

Gradually a pattern began to form in my life, get up, go to work, and go home to an empty house. At least the Spring brought warmer days, so I kept myself busy in the beautiful garden that had taken me over thirty years to create. I also had the joy of the two little girls that would bring me so much pleasure in the years that followed. However, there was an emptiness within me, as though all the things that were once so relevant seemed of no importance. The hundreds of CDs that I had played constantly were left in their sleeves, and my guitars remained hanging on the wall. June's death had taken away most of my interest in music, and sadly it was as though that part of my life had just gone.

For over a quarter of a century I had been lucky enough to be part of the boom years of Jersey's tourist trade. I had worked as a sales representative, and in the evening, I played guitar and sang in venues that were normally full. I was earning good money, doing something I enjoyed. All things end, and by the late 90s there had been a sharp decline in island visitors. Tourists were going elsewhere, and travel had become cheaper. Instead of families coming for a week or a fortnight, Jersey started to get Europeans coming for long weekends. Unlike the British, they hired cycles or wandered the island on foot. They were not people who went out much of an evening, content to have a pub meal and an early night. Whereas once I could be part of a duo or a band playing in venues for live music, one by one such places started to disappear. Those that remained started employing solo singers using taped backing tracks. The use of such recorded technology was not who I was but had become what the punters expected to hear. I made a few feeble attempts to keep up but was never comfortable and felt out of my depth. Gigs became few and far between. I had also reached my fifties and the carrying and setting up of heavy amps and big speakers was beginning to lose its charm. Audience attitudes had also changed, and people seemed less prone to listen. Payment had also dropped as disc jockeys were undercutting guys like me. I had made a lucrative addition to the family coffers over the years, that had also paid for wonderful holidays, but sadly the enjoyment had gone, and what was once pleasurable had become a job. So in the late 90s I called it a day. Music had become a chore, and in all honesty, I no longer needed the money.

In 2022 I left Jersey with Joanna and her family. Her husband Phil had originated from Somerset, where a large portion of his family still lived. It was decided that there was little future for their daughters on the island as neither wanted to go into the finance industry. I had said yes to joining them without hesitation because all my reasons for living in Jersey had gone. I now live quietly in Somerset, near to Joanna and her family. Stephen on the other hand has a successful business and his family group remain in Jersey. Foolishly through a mixture of loneliness and foolishness I had married someone totally unsuitable two and a half years after June's death. It was a huge mistake, and I eventually divorced her. I have few regrets however, as I believe all things happen for a reason and can help build character. That was ten years ago, and it's a period that has mostly been erased from my mind. Indeed, I'm older, a great deal wiser, and have the satisfaction of knowing that most of my life has been blessed. I will always believe that the first years of my life was the making of the man I became. What more could a kid from 'under the bridge' have asked for than to have had a wife who loved him without question, a life that blessed him with good parents, good children and lovely granddaughters, and a musical capability to make people happy? This 'mud man' has had quite an interesting ride since his birth in that tiny, terraced house 'under the bridge.' Shand Street, and the Garston of my childhood stays with me, and I remain proud to be a true 'mudman.'

AFTERWORD

Writing on the Wall (WoW) is an award-winning Liverpool-based community organisation, renowned for its celebration of writing in all its diverse forms. Hosting two dynamic festivals and a variety of year-round projects, WoW embraces literature, creative writing, journalism, poetry, songwriting and storytelling.

With a commitment to inclusivity, WoW collaborates with local, national, and international writers, providing invaluable opportunities for individuals to nurture their creativity and share their unique stories. Beyond its festivals and projects, WoW's creative writing initiatives serve as a catalyst for personal growth and community development, promoting health, wellbeing, and fostering connections across diverse communities.

Whether you're an experienced writer or embarking on your creative journey, WoW welcomes all who have a story to tell or a desire to explore the power of words.

Madeline Heneghan and Mike Morris
Co-Directors
www.writingonthewall.org.uk

273

JACK BYRNE

UNDER THE BRIDGE

BOOK ONE IN THE LIVERPOOL MYSTERIES SERIES

JACK BYRNE

ACROSS THE WATER

BOOK TWO IN THE LIVERPOOL MYSTERIES SERIES

JACK BYRNE

BEFORE THE STORM

BOOK THREE IN THE LIVERPOOL MYSTERIES SERIES

JACK BYRNE

BURNING DOWN THE HOUSE